Practical Policy Making and Job Description in Christian Ministry and Mission

ALLAN P. MILLER

B.Th., M. Min., D. R. Ed

Practical Policy Making and Job Description in Christian Ministry and Mission

Dr Allan P. Miller

Paperback Edition First Published in Great Britain in 2016
by aSys Publishing

eBook Edition First Published in Great Britain in 2016
by aSys Publishing

All Scriptures are from the King James Version of the Bible,
unless otherwise stated

ISBN: 978-1-910757-58-1
aSys Publishing 2016

Dedication

This study is dedicated specially to the membership and friends of Mount Calvary Church at the Birmingham branch England, where I have served as the host minister, from January 2015. You are one of my best friends and truly God's gifts to me! You have faithfully stood by me in the Ministry, in every challenge, from the beginning. To you all I owe a debt of gratitude for your ceaseless prayerful support and untiring efforts.

Contents

Acknowledgements

I feel an upmost sense of gratitude to the Almighty God, the Father of our Lord and Master Jesus Christ, through whose help and inspiration the vision for this book has become a fulfilment. I am also indebted to several "giants", upon whose shoulders I have stood, this making me "a little giant" in the fields of ministry, Christian leadership, book writing and mentoring. It is not possible to mention everyone in this acknowledgement, only a few will be mentioned here.

Thanks to The Most Rt. Rev Dr A. C. Evangelou, President of Ixthus Church Council, for writing the preface and also The Most Rt. Rev Dr M Lal – Director of Bethesda Biblical Institute of India - for the foreword. Thanks also to Rev Dr G. A. Christopher for his editorial work and valuable suggestions.

The following contributors – each of them is a highly responsible and respected scholar and clergy – deserve special appreciation: Dr Francis, Dr D. Henry, Dr P. Powell, Dr H. Henry, Dr G. Sackie-Osae, Dr Murray, Dr N. Taylor, Revd. Gomez, Revd. T. Burford, Dr I. Ojulalago, Dr J. Walker, and Prof John.

Last, but not the least, the diversity of the themes of this book and approaches offered here may contribute to a better understanding as well as expanded enrichment to us all the membership, friends and family of Mount Calvary Church, also to the Miller's families. Thanks to belief in me.

Preface

I t is an honour and privilege that it has been afforded to myself to be able to contribute a preface to Bishop Allan's new book entitled: "Practical Policy making and Job description in Christian Ministry and Mission". We are living in a time where Church principles, protocol and government are discarded and overlooked. Bishop Allan's book is a refreshing contribution to the Christian scholastic world. It is born from a life of experience and I believe places Bishop Allan among the wise men of the church, as Solomon tells us: He who walks with wise men will be wise, but the companion of fools will be destroyed {Proverbs 13:20 NAV}.

The book beautifully expounds on the role and responsibility of the different offices within the church, it gives a rich deep insight that will help the person who seeks to become that person whom God wants them to become. The book is theological and biblically based with excellent use of the appropriate Scriptures, the book is a signpost, at all times pointing and directing us to our Lord and Saviour Jesus Christ.

Bishop Miller is a true church man, at all times putting the wellbeing of the church above everything else. I commend him for such a wonderful insightful book and truly recommend it to all who desire the True Church. Bishop Allan always concerns about the standards of the church in general. Every member may not be invited to some special event, but every member is invited to attend to godly standards. When we raise the spiritual standards and immaturity gives way to maturity in Christian living, the innate conviction of dedicated lives will solve any spiritual problems we face when we have someone like Bishop Allan's looking at God for what is the next move for the church to take.

In conclusion I am privileged to call Bishop Miller a true co-worker in the Vineyard.

I remain with unending love and with special esteem

A.C. Evangelou, *BA, MA, D.D, MBE*

President of Ixthus Church Council

Bishop of Apostolic Christian Church

Foreword

I write the foreword to the book of Bishop Right Rev. Dr Allan P. Miller. The Book: "Practical Policy making and Job description in Christian Ministry and Mission" which is very useful for Christian churches, Leaders of Christian Ministries and Bible Colleges, Theological Colleges and Universities in the field of Theological, Biblical research studies and study of Pastoral Care.

In a day in which books about ministry and mission are being published at an unprecedented rate, there seems to be little evidence of their influence. I would suggest that this is not an ordinary book on "Practical Policy making and Job description in Christian Ministry and Mission" – nor does it convey a "fad" in current ministry and mission theory. Quite to the contrary, this remarkable volume focuses on the biblical and practical theology of job description.

This book is also very useful for the Christian Churches and Christian Institutions for the Development and growth of Church Ministry and Christian ministry. I have read the content and every Para of this book. I was feeling the presence of Holy Spirit. It was my feeling that God has guided the Honourable Man of God Dr Allan P. Miller to write this book through the guidance of the Holy Spirit for the Christian Churches and People of God. I know of no other book on practical policy which contains so much helpful and insightful information on the vital subject of authentic Christian ministry and mission.

I believe that our world desperately needs "Practical Policy making and Job description in Christian Ministry and Mission" who lead like Jesus Christ. The Scriptures teach us some very graphic and practical principles of ministry. Rev Dr Miller has grasped those vital principles. Bishop Right Rev Dr Allan P. Miller is a very anointed Man of God. I appreciate the work of Dr Allan P. Miller about his book. The material, content and para's of this book are amazing and wonderful. I hope that this book will be very useful in Christian World for the glory of our Lord Jesus Christ and extension of the kingdom of our Lord Jesus Christ around the world.

Mohan Lal, *B.Ed., B. Th., M.A., Ph. D*

Founder & President of Council of Bethesda Christian Church

Founder & Director of Bethesda Biblical Institute of India

Summary

My former studies, were aimed at providing a theological and historical background of the current reforms of liturgy through most Christian Churches. This present study aims at supplying a framework, also theological and historical, for research material by Christian individuals and groups for deeper and more personal understanding of God.

The purpose of this book is to identify those called into apostolic ministry and to help them function and fulfil their callings in their rightful places. By identifying and established the apostolic ministers in their place. As the mantle of apostle is a principality, so is the house founded, built, and covered by an apostle. The apostolic mantle on a person can translate to a mandate on his house. In truth, it is the house and its members that attest to the apostle's work, even beyond pastoral care, preaching and teaching, often leaves the minister (pastor) aware of his inability to be effective without the power of the Holy Spirit on his life.

Writing from the fact that there are at least three covering movements within the Christian church, which are evangelical which deals with the going out to the byways, prophetical which deals with the end time and apostolic which deals with correction, instruction and standard. This study book will be dealing with the apostolic movement which the Lord gave to use. Let me point out that the term "apostolic movement" or "apostolic leadership" has nothing to do with Jesus Only Church / or Oneness Church. This is where we have the most problems. It is difficult for most churches that are part of this corporate house to recognize other churches and individuals that have an apostolic calling or an apostolic mantle.

When you look at the evangelical movement as a whole, there are some that don't believe that there are apostles, prophets and teachers. So they don't design their churches after the five-fold ministry. Some use pastors and deacon, pastors and elders or pastors, elders, and deacons, the gifting of a prophet or on evangelist are not recognized. Whether in the Old Testament or New Testament, ministry finds its meaning and expression in Jesus Christ. He is the Minister par excellence and the only source of ministry. It is reasonably clear in Scripture that (1) ministry means the service of God and his creatures; (2) the one essential ministry is that of Jesus Christ; (3) the whole membership of the old and the new Israel is called to share in ministerial service, of which there are many forms.

The first responsibility God has given the pastoral ministry is to watch over the flock. The idea is one of spiritual alertness, being on the watch, being ready. This ministry was designed to be effective, penetrating, prophetic and life –giving; and those who were called to deliver it, were called to be a people with a Biblical lifestyle. The manner of the apostle's ministry is a paradoxical mixture of honour and dishonour. He is a chosen representative of Jesus Christ according to God's will and decree (1 Corinthians 1:1). Every person who is called by God is given a destination dream (vision). It is a dream that pales everything else into insignificance. While it is true that renewal is necessary, nowhere does it remove the responsibility from the human being to decide at each point either not to believe, or to keep believing God.

It is the responsibility of every generation of Christians to discover, understand, interpret and own afresh the timeless truths of the Word of God. In relation to Christ every member of Israel or the Church has a ministry of serving the Lord by proclaiming the Word of God by word and deed both inside and outside the people of God. When, even the instruments of ministry are broken and panic strikes the heart, we should simply trust in God and His unchanging promises. Further, in relation to Christ, there are specific or particular forms of ministry within and for the sake of the Church in its mission for God in this world. How an individual responds to the mission and message is critically decisive?

The major audience in mind is the person who is already in a place of Church leadership or who is anticipating a leadership responsibility. Persons in either category would be continuing students of administrative leadership. Pastors, other Church ministers, Church leaders in general, and many who minister in other agencies which exist to assist Churches should find this text useful. The source of much of this text is the local congregation, and it is experience oriented. Indeed, readers will recognize that I have participated in the life and ministry of churches for a number of years. In several places in this volume I use my own ministerial organizational patterns of Mount Calvary Church as examples and models of how the tasks of Church administration might be fulfilled within the various ministries of a local Church. I hope you will be helped by these suggestions.

This research has demonstrated that the pursuit of training in Ministry and Theology is necessary for the intellectual, moral and spiritual growth the Christian Community. And I have nothing to do with my former church fellowship namely: Mount Calvary Holy Church of America, but just and only the ministry that the Lord gave me namely: Mount Calvary Holy Church and the Mount Calvary Church from 2011 that has been used as examples within this book. The apostolic ministry movement consists of men of God who are called as apostles in cities, regions, national and international, who have an accredited word, and be willing to stand behind that word, and flow with it! We need to begin to pray that the Christian leaders of those ministries will communicate, collaborate, pray together, share information, and be united concerning the vision for the city and for the nation, so that we can weaken the force and the power of the demonic thrust in that city.

Allan P, Miller, *B. Th., M. Min., D. R. Ed*

Host Minister: Birmingham Branch Mount Calvary Church

Bishop of Mount Calvary Church, England and Wales

Member of Ixthus Church Council, International based in the UK

Chapter One

Job Description in Pastoral Management

Apostolic ministries are usually different from the normal conventional churches that are established in cities or urban. They are essentially impartation ministries, and many will drive far and near to receive strategy and impartation from direct proportion to the assignments, the mantle, and the mission that has been given to apostolic covering. It is very important to understand that the emphasis of the anointing and influence that is released from a ministry is based on the anointing that has been given and apportioned to the resident apostolic man or woman that is divinely placed over the ministry (church). No apostolic ministry can function beyond the influence and anointing of its apostolic leadership. As the anointing and influence of a ministry grows, the anointing and influence will begin to develop men and women in God's calling.

Job description is meant to define and describe an assignment and the scope of the work to be done. It is normally used in the secular realm in management. It is also used in the church today, to maximize effectiveness of ministry. Job description in pastoral ministry is not a recent development; it was used by Moses, in response to Jethro's admonition. In his counsel to Moses, Jethro said:

Hearken now unto my voice, I will give thee counsel, and God shall be with thee: Be thou for the people to Godward, that thou mayest bring the causes unto God: and thou shalt teach them ordinances and laws, and shalt show them the way wherein they must walk, and the work that they must do {Exodus 18:19-20AV}.

In verse 20, Jethro advised Moses to show the people "the work that they must do". That is, to define and describe their assignments and their scope of authority to function.

1

This should explain what the person does and the scope of their ministry in the church organisation. For example, Sunday School Superintendent, Youth Department Coordinator, Teacher, Assistant Pastor, etc. Here the specific responsibilities are listed. For the sake of clarity, first the broadest groupings of responsibilities should be listed, and then under each of these detailed responsibilities, the leader should explain what must be done within the grouping. Sometimes these callings might be different from the original ministry (church) calling, even though they are birthed from the same apostolic ministry. Often these men and women begin to develop their own emphasis and influence in preparation for their own ministry and, like the ministry they were raised in, they begin to influence cities and nations also.

Because each leader's responsibility calls for a degree of authority, the next thing that needs to be described is:

The levels of authority of each personnel

1. Act without informing—here the individual can fulfil his responsibility on his own initiative. He or she does not have to inform his or her Superior (Pastor, Bishop, or Manager) nor seek approval for his or her actions.

2. Act and Inform—here the individual can feed his or her responsibility on his own initiative, but he should inform his Superior (Pastor, Bishop, or Manager) of the results of his actions.

3. Act after Approval—here the individual does not act until the Pastor or Manager has given approval. He may have to do some research or preliminary planning, for example, of or introducing a strategy or methodology in developing his Department. In such cases actions may only be taken after approval. On the other hand the more experienced a person is the more authority should be given them to act.

Working relationship

In the Parable of the Talents, we are told that after the Master had given the talents to the three men, according to their several abilities, he left them to develop their talents, each person using his own initiative.

Again, it will be like a man going on a journey, who called his servants and entrusted his property to them. To one he gave five talents of money, to another two talents, and to another one talent, each according to his ability. Then he went on his journey. The man who had received the five talents went at once and put his money to work and gained five more. So also, the one with the two talents gained two more. But the man who had received the one talent went off, dug a hole in the ground and hid his master's money (Matthew 25:14-18 NIV).

He did not attempt to coerce each person, nor did he attempt to encroach into the individual's freedom and delegated authority to act in the best interest of the master. In addition to what has been said above, there must be a well-established structure, put in place to define the level and limits of authority, within the organisation. This is necessary to avoid chaos or ecclesiastical anarchy, which result from a situation where each person claims to be the "boss". Such a situation will undermine the office and authority of the Pastor and cause confusion within the Church. This was the state of Israel, after the death of Samson.

In those days there was no king in Israel: every man did that which was right in his own eyes (Judges 21:25 AV).

To avoid such occurrence, every officer must know his level of responsibility and authority. Paul instructs that everything must be done "in decency and in order" (1 Corinthians 14:40). Jothro's management counsel to Moses clearly defines each officer's level of authority; every sub leader knew his scope of leadership, to whom he was responsible and who was responsible to him.

And Mount Sinai was altogether on a smoke, because the Lord descended upon it in fire: and the smoke thereof ascended as the smoke of a furnace, and the whole mount quaked greatly. And when the voice of the trumpet sounded long, and waxed louder and louder, Moses spake, and God answered him by a voice. And the Lord came down upon Mount Sinai, on the top of the mount: and the Lord called Moses up to the top of the mount; and Moses went up. And the Lord said unto Moses, Go down, charge the people, lest they break through unto the Lord to gaze, and many of them perish. And let the priests also, which come near to the Lord, sanctify themselves, lest the Lord break forth upon them (Exodus 18:15-22 AV).

3

In the light of the above, I would like to suggest these four points:

1. Whom does a Pastor report to? To the Senior Pastor or District Pastor or the Bishop!

2. Who reports to the Pastor? The Head of every Department in the Local Church!

3. Who reports to the Team Leaders or Departmental Head? Every member of that team in the local Church!

4. With whom must I work closely? With the rest of the Pastoral Team, with the Management Teams, with the Faith of the Local Church?

Delegation in Organisation

Delegation is the process of entrusting authority and responsibility to others in a way which enables them to makes the same decision as the Pastor or Bishop will do in effectiveness of the same Local Church. If any Church fails to use the principles of delegation this can lead to confusion, frustration and dwindling effectiveness. Delegation relieves you of burdens that can he shouldered by others (Exodus 18:19-27). Delegation helps you spend more time planning for the future (Number 11:10-25). Delegation will result in an increase of the total amount of work accomplished.

Jethro made this strong reason for delegation: Let them serve as judges for the people on a permanent basis. They can bring all the difficult cases to you, but they themselves can decide all the smaller disputes. That will make it easier for you, as they share your burden. If you do this as God commands, you will not wear yourself out, and all these people can go home with their disputes settled (Exodus 18:22-23 GNV).

The apostles saw the benefits of delegation, not only in relation to the Churches as a whole, but in relation to themselves; they needed more time to pray, study and plan.

Therefore, friends, look out seven men of good reputation from your number, men full of the Spirit and of wisdom, and we will appoint them to deal with these matters, while we devote ourselves to prayer and to the ministry of the Word (Acts 6:3-4 NEV).

If a leader does not delegate, he will tend to carry all the burdens, and make all the decisions alone. This may be because of many personal weaknesses within that minister. Lack of delegation can make members of the local Church inactive and dormant, and as a result they may lose their motivation or become uncooperative.

For God is not the author of confusion, but of peace, as in all Churches of the saints (1 Corinthians 14:33 AV).

Pastors reasons for not delegating

Delegating involves a threat, for the person to whom you are delegating may be able to do it better than you are able to do it. It may tend to make you feel as though you are losing touch with the task. This needs not be the case. (2 Samuel 5:17-23) Delegating never releases the Pastor, Bishop or Manager from carrying the ultimate responsibility. Moreover, it helps you to focus and spend more time on the most important aspects of the ministry, which only you can do best. Thus, you can maximize your effectiveness.

Fear is the root cause of lack of delegation. Fear of losing one's authority, losing touch with the people, fear of losing one's recognition and reputation. These fears are totally unfounded, where a leader knows his calling. In a few instances there have been cases of rebellion against leadership, from delegated subordinates. This is to be expected, where over ambition and unfaithfulness are present. Examples include Korah and his cohorts (Num. 16:1-35), Alexander the coppersmith (1Timothy 1:19-20; 2 Timothy 4:14-16) Hymeneous and Philetus (1Timothy 1:20; 2 Timothy 2: 17-18).

These negative examples, not withstanding, a leader should not feel threatened. He should be courageous to put capable men in offices, as long as he is truly called of God and as long as he himself is faithful to his calling. It is always better to delegate, than not to delegate.

Many ministries would have continued today, if the leaders had prayerfully delegated authority. Because they chose not to delegate, many prosperous ministries of yester years have died with their founders. God instructed Moses to groom Joshua for leadership. Moses was to lay his hands upon Joshua, so that he might transfer some of his power to Joshua (Deuteronomy 34:9).

The work of God did not cease when Moses died; it was continued by Joshua, Moses anointed successor (Joshua 1:1-8). Because administrative and organisational structures were in place!

Now after the death of Moses the servant of the LORD it came to pass, that the LORD spake unto Joshua the son of Nun, Moses minister, saying, Moses my servant is dead; now therefore arise, go over this Jordan, thou, and all this people, unto the land which I do give to them, even to the children of Israel. Every place that the sole of your foot shall tread upon, that have I given unto you, as I said unto Moses. From the wilderness and this Lebanon even unto the great river, the river Euphrates, all the land of the Hittites, and unto the great sea toward the going down of the sun, shall be your coast. There shall not any man be able to stand before thee all the days of thy life: as I was with Moses, so I will be with thee: I will not fail thee, nor forsake thee. Be strong and of a good courage: for unto this people shalt thou divide for an inheritance the land, which I sware unto their fathers to give them. Only be thou strong and very courageous, that thou mayest observe to do according to all the law, which Moses my servant commanded thee: turn not from it to the right hand or to the left, that thou mayest prosper whithersoever thou goest. This book of the law shall not depart out of thy mouth; but thou shalt meditate therein day and night, that thou mayest observe to do according to all that is written therein: for then thou shalt make thy way prosperous, and then thou shalt have good success (Joshua 1:1-8 AV).

Today Apostles, Prophets, Evangelists, Pastors, Deacons, Elders, Bishop and Teachers across the land are crying out for a man like Joshua to come to their aid. From this definition we see that Joshua's duty was to wait on Moses. Moses was willing to invest his anointing, and his whole life, into Joshua. He was willing to relinquish control and allow Joshua to take the people into the Promised Land, even though Moses had personally shepherded the people for forty years in the wilderness. He knew that the children of Israel belonged to God, not to him. The point I intend to enforce here is that the Church is not the minister's property, it is the Lord's. The minister is only a steward, a caretaker that is a manager employed by God. He should see himself as someone who would someday be called to give account of his stewardship to God. Moses knew that the children of Israel belonged to God, not to himself; he was only an instrument in Jehovah's hand. Thus, he was flexible enough to invest into his successor.

Paul delegated Titus to the Island of Crete, as the first bishop of that island. Titus was given a specific mandate: to reorganise the seemingly disorganised assemblies and to appoint Church leaders in every city to manage the affairs of the assemblies in their cities.

The reason I left you in Crete was that you might straighten out what was left unfinished and appoint elders in every town, as I directed you. An elder must be blameless, the husband of but one wife, a man whose children believe and are not open to the charge of being wild and disobedient. Since an overseer is entrusted with God's work, he must be blameless—not overbearing, not quick-tempered, not given to much wine, not violent, not pursuing dishonest gain. Rather he must be hospitable, one who loves what is good, who is self-controlled, upright, holy and disciplined. He must hold firmly to the trustworthy message as it has been taught, so that he can encourage others by sound doctrine and refute those who oppose it (Titus 1:5-9 NIV).

Qualification of team members

Church leaders need to do their duties effectively. To do this, there is the need for them to know the art of some communicating skills. I am fully convinced that the Lord has called me, with a specific mandate for this end time. That mandate is to reach people for Christ.

I found in the communication process, there are four primary elements:

1. The Transmitter, is the preacher
2. The Message, is the gospel
3. The Channel, is the words
4. The Receivers, are the people to whom we want to convey the Christian message of God's love and power.

The duties of leaders are both a science and an art. Thus, preaching is not an act, not just a show, or a circus neither should it be 'dullsville', a tranquilliser or sleepy time. It must have good taste in order to prevail. In preaching to young people especially, no creative stone should be left unturned in presenting the gospel. The message should be presented in an interesting, informative and inspiring way.

A team that spends time planning and organising usually is delighted to be involved in launching this project. Through proper control the leader can keep the project alive. Through feedback he can maintain the level of enthusiasm and read just the goals.

This is why I believe that no manager or Pastor has the ability to make every decision a perfect decision. No manager or pastor has the ability to draw up a plan that never needs to be adjusted. Managing makes it possible to see, at an early stage, when a plan needs to be changed. Through accurate feedback, a minister is able to make the right adjustments. As he compares the action with the actual results and the original plan he will be able to see the areas that needs to be adjusted and better equipped to understand and know how to equip and rescue others.

Paul wrote to Timothy: You heard my teaching in the presence of many witnesses; put that teaching into the charge of men you can trust, such men as will be competent to teach others (2 Timothy 2:2 NEV).

Timothy was to "commit" responsibility to "faithful men" who will, in turn, teach others. Paul used the Greek word "Paratithemi", meaning to "deposit", to place alongside. It conveys the idea of delegation. Managing in some sense is like counselling. This is the link between the two, the leader as a counsellor and subordinate as a counselee.

Team counselling is an attempt to provide encouragement and guidance for those facing situations that they are unsure about, unfamiliar or feel they cannot cope with. In managing a team the pastor aims at helping the team to cope more effectively with problems, or boost their inner confidence or lift their inner conflict.

The Spirit of Unity in Managing the Church

This is a persistent problem in any Church, and the solution requires some counselling skills in the recognition of individual differences among members, and the ability to help each person accept his or her own strengths and weaknesses. A timely presentation of incentives to saints and ministers of differing sentiments and the abilities to make them work together demands wise application of management and counselling methodologies. I will be clarifying some issues for deliberation, which will bring some changes.

The unity of an effective ministry is brought about by the Spirit of God working and not though family blood. However, the Holy Spirit does not enforce unity to unwilling believers. Both the members and leaders of the local Church must cooperate with the Holy Spirit, to maintain this unity. Paul wrote to the Corinthians:

By the authority of our Lord Jesus Christ I appeal to all of you, my brothers, to agree in what you say, so that there will be no divisions among you. Be completely united, with only one thought and one purpose. For some people from Chloe's family have told me quite plainly, my brothers, that there are quarrels among you. Let me put it this way: each one of you says something different one says, "I follow Paul"; another, "I follow Apollos"; another, "I follow Peter"; and another, "I follow Christ". Christ has been divided into groups! Was it Paul who died on the cross for you? Were you baptized as Paul's disciples? (1 Corinthians 1:10-13 GNV)

The Church cannot function in unity, without the Holy Spirit. The disciples had been selfish about their individual concerns, until the Spirit descended on the Day of Pentecost. The coming of the Holy Spirit formed the New Testament Church into a unified, mystical and spiritual organism. To keep the unity perpetuated, the Church must be in "one accord". This was what happened on the Day of Pentecost. They were "in one accord" and together "in one place".

And when the day of Pentecost was fully come, they were all with one accord in one place. And suddenly there came a sound from heaven as of a rushing mighty wind, and it filled all the house where they were sitting. And there appeared unto them cloven tongues like as of fire, and it sat upon each of them. And they were all filled with the Holy Ghost, and began to speak with other tongues, as the Spirit gave them utterance (Acts 2:1-4 AV).

The Holy Spirit initiates and perpetuates this unity in the Body of Christ. Thus, we become "one Body", though many members. In this dispensation, unity can be maintained through God's ordained leadership. The five-fold ministries are God's ordained instruments for maintaining this unity.

In his epistle to the Ephesians, Paul wrote: And he gave some, apostles; and some, prophets; and some, evangelists; and some, pastors and teachers; For the perfecting of the saints, for the work of the ministry, for the edifying of the body of Christ: Till we all come in the unity of the faith, and of the knowledge of the Son of God, unto a perfect man, unto the measure of the stature of the fullness of Christ: That we henceforth be no more children, tossed to and fro, and carried about with every wind of doctrine, by the sleight of men, and cunning craftiness, whereby they lie in wait to deceive (Ephesians 4:11-14 AV).

Peter's preaching on the Day of Pentecost was gladly supported by the other apostles. They stood up with him, in the spirit of unity while he ministered the word.

But Peter, standing up with the eleven, lifted up his voice, and said unto them, Ye men of Judaea, and all ye that dwell at Jerusalem, be this known unto you, and hearken to my words (Acts 2:14 AV).

In Matthew 12:25, Jesus taught that a "house divided against itself", cannot stand. Unity is the secret of spiritual strength in the Church. Unity releases the Spirit and power of God, giving the believers the liberty to express themselves in a truly united and spiritual atmosphere; for "where the Spirit of God is, there is liberty". Unity makes the presence of God to be felt and gives access to kingdom authority.

And I say also unto thee, that thou art Peter, and upon this rock I will build my Church; and the gates of hell shall not prevail against it. And I will give unto thee the keys of the kingdom of heaven: and whatsoever thou shalt bind on earth shall be bound in heaven: and whatsoever thou shalt loose on earth shall be loosed in heaven. Then charged he his disciples that they should tell no man that he was Jesus the Christ (Matthew 16: 18-20 AV).

Many liked the eloquence and the miraculous powers of Paul. However, Paul did not cater for the "sin of denominationalism", but he was much more concerned about the schism, division and the party spirit prevailing in the Church of Corinthians (1 Corinthians 1:10-12). There are times in Church life when there are disagreements concerning doctrines and practices, the Apostolic Church certainly had their share (see Ephesians 4:3 and 13 and 1Corinthians 12:25).

How can we recognise the spirit of unity in the Church? Unity is what we can sense, see and feel. Paul used the human body as a metaphor to illustrate how unity works in the Church. As Christians, we are all members of one body, the body of Christ. So, like in the physical body, whatever happens to any part of the Body, no matter how little that part may appear to be, the whole body will feel it. This is how we know unity exists.

For the body is not one member, but many. If the foot shall say, because I am not the hand, I am not of the body; is it therefore not of the body? And if the ear shall say, because I am not the eye, I am not of the body; is it therefore not of the body? If the whole body were an eye, where were the hearing? If the whole were hearing, where were the smelling? But now hath God set the members every one of them in the body, as it hath pleased him. And if they were all one member, where were the body? But now are they many members, yet but one body. And the eye cannot say unto the hand, I have no need of thee: nor again the head to the feet, I have no need of you (1 Corinthians 12: 14-21 AV).

When my toes are stepped on, my whole body screams out in pain. When my eyes are delighted, my heart excites the whole body. The early Christians went to prison together, they suffered together, they walked together, they believed together, they prayed together, they sang together, and they shall all reign together.

The Apostles inspire and lead ways to fresh and earnest desire for Jesus. They are also the foundation layers of the Church. The Prophets are the inspired teachers of the word. Prophets speak by direct divine inspiration and revelation. Evangelists remind us of the lost. They are anointed to preach and get people saved. Pastors are God's Shepherds, who care for God's sheep. Teachers have divine ability to teach and establish people the Word of God.

Let us study Paul's life in Romans 15: 20. He stayed six months to three years in each place, long enough to establish people in the (Ministry) or the Church. The individual may ask: Do I have the ability to provide adequate Spiritual Leadership in the (Ministry) or Church from the time I have been in (Ministry) or Church?

Minister & Reverend Licensing that Mount Calvary Church will be using

The following risk management questions has been designed to help churches in effective. It is designed and adopted by our Church—Mount Calvary Church—and I believe it will be useful to other churches and ministries.

11

1. What is your occupation besides the ministry?

2. How long have you been in the ministry?

3. How often do you attend your local church each week?

4. What auxiliaries do you belong to in your local church?

5. What is the extent of your education?

6. What is the extent of your Christian walk?

7. What are your plans to further develop your skills?

8. What training do you have in Biblical Studies and or the Ministry?

9. Describe the relationship you share with your Senior Pastor

10. Describe the various duties you perform in your local church?

11. Describe your call to the ministry?

12. Describe your Pentecostal experience including your ministry gift?

13. What is the work of a Minister / Reverend as it relates to a "local preacher?

14. What is the difference between the expression saved, sanctified, baptised, and filled with the Holy Ghost?

15. What is the significance of tithing?

16. Is it important to belong to a Church? Why or why not?

17. What is the significance of the fruit of the Spirit?

18. Interpret in your own words—2 Timothy 2:15

19. Interpret in your own words—Hebrew 12:14

20. Interpret in your own words—2 Corinthians 5:17

21. What is the significance of your local church?

22. What is the significance of the whole Armour of God?

23. What is sin?

24. What is the significance of preaching? 26. What is a text?

25. What is the "Great Commandment? And where is it found in the Bible?

26. What is the significance of St John 3:16?

27. What is the work of a "soul—winner?

28. What do you know about the "heritage of church organisation?

29. Identify the following Biblical personalities:

- Abraham, Isaac, and Jacob
- Moses
- Ahab
- Elijah's and Elisha
- Nicodemus
- Philemon
- Demas
- John the Baptist, and John the Beloved
- Elizabeth
- Legion
- Caleb

30. Identify the following Biblical places—what happened here?

- Cana of Galilee
- The Pool of Bethesda
- Golgotha
- The Mount of Olives
- Capernaurn
- 31. Quote from memory the following Biblical expressions:
- Five of the Ten Commandments
- Five of the Beatitudes
- Five of the Parable of Jesus.

Contributor

D r Allan Miller's book: "Practical Policy Making and Job Description in Christian Ministry and Mission" is a timely book, an invaluable aid for Pastors and Church leaders. It has been written as result of Dr Miller's passion to share his profound wealth of knowledge—theological and experiential—to a wider audience, particularly, the Afro-Caribbean Pentecostal Community.

In thirteen powerful chapters, Dr Miller challenges Church leaders to rise up to their God-given mandate of Shepherding. He articulates with boldness, the need for a change in the philosophy and practice of Church leadership, in view of the "Knowledge Explosion" which has characterized this End Times.

Dr Miller has demonstrated, with great skill and precision, that: spirituality and scholarship, theology and faith, success and sanctity, education and missionary activities, character and charisma, are coexistent; they constitute a healthy balance for excellence in ministry and mission. Thus, he has proved to be erroneous, the traditional philosophy of ministry that has prevailed in the Pentecostal Community for decades.

As a wise 'physician', the writer has not only 'diagnosed' and exposed the flaws of the Church and her leadership, he has 'prescribed' the cures, based on well researched biblical principles, historical evidences and contemporary examples. He has done so with confidence derived from his theological convictions, scholarly acumen, purity of motive and practicable guideline.

I have had the singular privilege to have read Dr Miller's work in the original form and the present volume—several times over. I am convinced that it is a timely book for Church leaders. It should be used for Church ministry, as a text book for theological students and a manual for preachers, both young and old. Dr Miller has done a noble work, for this, I congratulate him.

G. A. Christopher, Ph. D., D. D., Litt. D

General Overseer: World Missionary Gospel Church

Lagos, Nigeria: West Africa

Chapter Two

Understanding Christian Ministry

Ministry is essentially serving God through meeting the needs of others. It is building the Body of Christ by using the spiritual gifts and talents given to us by the Lord. For example, Jesus came to minister. His ministry involved teaching about the Kingdom of God, healing the sick and communicating with His heavenly Father in prayer. His whole life was dedicated to serving others. He also stresses integrity, duty, service, and diligence, with sacrifice being the heart of what it He taught and expected His disciples to do. You can recognize it by its constant cry for excellence, wisdom and maturity. His ministers are usually grounded and mature, and form a network of potent partners and warriors that keep their territory primarily clear, and the blessings of God flowing uninterrupted into the earth.

What is the Purpose of a Ministry?

In his epistle to the Church in Ephesus, Apostle Paul wrote about the purpose and functions of the five-fold ministries in the church. He said:

And he gave some, apostles; and some, prophets; and some, evangelists; and some, pastors and teachers; for the perfecting of the saints, for the work of the ministry, for the edifying of the body of Christ {Ephesus 4:11-12 AV}.

The early pastors were very effective in their calling. This effectiveness reflected in the lives of the people under their pastoral care. Because of their effectiveness, most of the early Christians were well learned in the Word of God, mature in Spirit, consistent in character and well equipped for ministry—both in their local assemblies and in their worldwide ministries. This is how the church is to be empowered through pastoral leadership.

The purpose of any New Testament church ministry is threefold:

1. Perfecting the saints or to prepare and establish believers in God's work.
2. Equipping the saints which means:
3. To fully prepare and build the entire Body of Christ throughout the Word.
4. To lead the church to complete unity of faith in the Body of Christ.
5. To bring to maturity the Body of Christ.
6. Building up or edifying the Body of Christ or to bring the Body to the full measure of the fullness of Christ.

To be effective in fulfilling this purpose, ministers need the power of the Holy Spirit. Jesus has promised to give us this "dunamis" {power} to help us do God's work supernaturally (see Acts 1:8). For the work of God is not accomplished by human power or wisdom, but by the Spirit of God {Zech.4:6}.

God has called all believers to the ministry of power. It is through this power that we are able to overthrow the kingdom of the enemy and establish God's work in our midst. The ministry of Jesus was successful because it was packed with power and spiritual authority. The disciples were uneducated common people, but their ministry was marked with power and authority. They made a difference in their time because they had the power. God has made this power available to all his servants because without it we will accomplish little. One can be Spirit-filled but lack power! I have met a lot of powerless Spirit-filled believers. What does it take to have the kind of power I am talking about? It takes prayer, faith, fasting and regular study of the Word of God.

Ministerial Workers

The term "worker" is a designation used in Christian ministry or Church fellowship for anyone who is called, appointed or delegated to serve God and His people is His vineyard. Anyone who serves in any capacity, at any level in the Church, is a "Ministerial Worker". Any service we render to God and other Christians, within the context of the Church, is a "ministry".

The term "worker" has been borrowed from the secular concepts of workmanship, where a "worker" is viewed as an employee, a labourer or a craftsman. A ministerial worker, then, is a believer who is appointed to serve—either directly called or chosen by God or appointed through the leadership of the local Church. A ministerial worker may also be called a "helper", "an assistant", "a servant", a "labourer", or "a minister"—because he or she is involved in Church service, work or ministry.

There are different kinds of workmanship and there are different levels of ministry in the local Church—depending on your calling, level of anointing, office, experience or maturity. Generally, workers in the local Church setting are delegated and empowered by the leadership of the Church. Therefore, the following can be designated as "Ministerial Workers".

1. Overseers / Bishop
2. Pastors
3. Elders
4. Deacons
5. Sunday School Teachers
6. Choir Leaders
7. Prayer Band Leaders
8. Missionary Band Leaders
9. Evangelism Team Leaders
10. Women's Leaders
11. Men's Leaders
12. Youth Team Leaders
13. Other Church Officials:
    a. Ushers
    b. Treasurers
    c. Secretaries, etc.,

Some Christians have objected to the use of "worker" in the Church. They would rather like to be called "Church officials" or "ministers". They feel that the use of "worker" is more secular than spiritual; that it tends to make the Christian worker "a hired man" or a "hireling" or an employee who only serves the leadership. The use of "worker" is not indemnifying for those who labour or serve God in the Church.

Every worker is personally accountable to God. He or she may have been delegated or appointed by the Church leadership, to serve under the supervision of the Church leadership, the worker is expected to serve as though he or she were directly employed by God; "with singleness of heart, as unto Christ", "not with eye service, as men pleasers; but as servants of Christ, doing the will of God from the heart; with good will doing service, as to the Lord, and not to men". (Eph.6:5-7; cp.Col.3:22) and "willingly", in the fear of God (1 Peter 5:5-7)

And whatsoever ye do, do it heartily, as to the Lord, and not unto men; knowing that of the Lord ye shall receive the reward of the inheritance; for ye service the Lord Jesus Christ. But he that doeth wrong shall receive the wrong which he hath done; and there is no respect of persons (Col.3:22-23; cp.Eph.6:7-8)

Greek Terms for Workers

Several words are used in the New Testament for those who serve in the Lord's Vineyard.

The most commonly used word is ergates {from ergon—work}. This word means "labourer", "workman" and "worker".

a. It is translated workers in Luke 13:27—workers {of iniquity}. Philp.3:2—"evil" {workers. 2 Corinthians 11:13—{deceitful} workers.

b. Workman in Matt.10:10 "workman is worthy of his meat". In the Revived Version, it is "labourer". It is also used in 2 Tim.2:15 as "workman".

Study to shew thyself approved unto God, a workman that needeth not to be ashamed, rightly dividing the word of truth (2 Timothy 2:15 AV)

As we can see in this context, the work man or worker is in reference to a preacher or minister of the word. It is translated "workman" in Acts 19:25, of non-Christian workers or workers in the secular realm. This implies that ministry is "work" and a minister is a "worker". Paul admonished Timothy to "do the work of an Evangelist make full proof of thy ministry" (2 Timothy 4:5). Again, as we can see, "the work of an Evangelist" is a "ministry". Thus, an Evangelist is "a worker" as well as a "minister".

Nehemiah describes his ministry as "a great work".

And I sent messengers unto them saying, I am doing a great work, so that I cannot come down: why should the work cease, whilst I leave it, and come down to you? (Nehemiah 6:3 AV).

He describes his fellow workers and builders as people who had "a mind to work".

So build we the wall; and all the wall was joined together unto the half there of: for the people had a mind to work (Nehemiah 4:6 AV).

c. The word is also translated "labourer" or "labourers". "The harvest is plenteous, but the labourers are few" (Matt.9:37 AV). Pray that God will send forth labourers into this harvest" (Matt. 9:38 AV). The harvest truly is great but the labourers are few . . . that he would send labourers into his harvest (Luke 10:2). For the labourer is worthy of his hire (Luke 10:7). The labourer is worthy of his reward (1 Tim.5:18); See also: Matt.20:1, 2, 8; Jam.5:4).

Paul wrote about Christian workers who led and guided the Church in Thessalonica.

And we beseech you, brethren, to know them which labour among you, and are over you in the Lord, and admonish you; and to esteem them highly in love for their work's sake (1 Thess.5:12-13 AV).

Paul also spoke of workers who "labour in word and in doctrine" (1 Tim.5:17), who are "worthy of double honour". Paul teaches that, while we are all "workers" or "labourers" in the field of souls, there are some labourers among us who "are over us in the Lord". We should "know" or recognize such key workers and "esteem them highly", or accord them "double honour" for the work they are doing.

Church Work as a Team Ministry

Team ministry is when two or more people with ministry gifts join efforts to work together for the common good. God's pattern is for different ministries to work together in a team to bring the Body of Christ into perfection. He wants each ministry to compliment and support the others to form a complete unity (1 Peter 4:10-11).

Naturally, some people are too insecure to raise up others in ministry or to take time to work with others. Some ministers would even live longer if they raised up supportive ministries. We should work together because we serve the same Master; we are citizens of the same Kingdom and labourers in the same vineyard. God intends for us to work with each other as a team in building His Kingdom. The Bible says, "two are better than one" {Eccl.4:9) and "iron sharpens iron" {Prov.27:17}. A person who works alone never grows and overcomes his or her weaknesses. He has no one to correct him or her when he is wrong or help him or her when he needs help. He never learns to overcome the spirit of jealousy, insecurity and selfishness unless he learns to work with others.

Every member needs to be functional in his place for the Body to be healthy. The local church leadership has a great responsibility to use its offices for the purpose of equipping the saints for the work of ministry. This is the only way to build the Body of Christ (Eph.4:11-12). Team ministry helps to multiply our efforts and results. It helps us to increase our potential and make more disciples for Christ.

Team spirit creates a positive, healthy and spiritual environment where the ministry can succeed. It creates a suitable atmosphere for the Spirit to work among and bless God's people. On the Day of Pentecost, all the apostles "were in one accord". And the Holy Spirit came down to bless, anoint and empower the church {Act 2:1-4}. When Peter stood up to minister, all the other apostles stood up to support him—the ministration of Peter produced miraculous effects {see: Acts 2:14-17}. It is only when "Paul Plants" and "Apollos waters" that God can give the increase {1 Cor.3:6-8}.

All the compound designations for Church workmanship, "fellow workers", "fellow helper", "workers together", etc., can be summed up as "team ministry". In a team ministry, every worker is a member of the team. Every member of the team is an important team member. The team ministry is like a football team, where no player is totally independent or isolated; every player cooperates with other members of his team to achieve the collective objective of the team—that is to score goals and win the game. It does not matter who scores the goal, every member rejoices and shares in the success. To make team ministry effective, I suggest that:

a. Every worker must be willing to subordinate his / her personal agenda to the wider vision or goal or mission of the team. No team member is bigger than the team as a whole.

b. Every worker must cooperate with and support the leadership of the team—just as team players are expected to submit to their team captain. While everyone is a "player", not everyone is the captain; there can only be one captain in the team.

c. Every worker must be a faithful ambassador of the team.

d. Every worker must maintain a team spirit and promote a team effort. This is necessary because:

  » A tree cannot make a forest; no man is an island to himself. In Church ministry, we all need one another.

  » The Church cannot survive where there is no team effort.

  » A kingdom divided against itself cannot stand; a Church where workers are divided and uncooperative will not fulfil its vision (See: Matt.12:25).

  » No one can succeed without the help or support of others; two are always better than one (See: Eccl.4:9-10).

  » As a member of the team, you rise when the team succeeds and you fall when it falls. The rising or falling of your team depends on you. Therefore, serve well and play your role faithfully.

  » Therefore, to fulfil your role as a worker or team member in the Church, you must:

  » Maintain the unity in the Body of Christ (Eph. 4).

  » Cooperate with other team members and submit yourself to your team leader.

  » Harmonize your vision with that of the team. The team is bigger than you alone; you cannot succeed, without working with, not against, your team.

- » Love and appreciate other members of the team.
- » Endeavour to "be at peace with all" the members of the team (See: Heb.12:4).

Examples of team ministry abound in the Bible. The following are a few examples.

1. The battle of Israel against the Amalekites

The battle of Israel against the Amalekites at Engadi, is an excellent example of a team effort. There was perfect unity and cooperation among everyone involved. While Joshua led his men in the war, Moses' stood on top of the hill, with his rod lifted up to God in prayer. As long as Moses' hands remained steady upward, Joshua was winning the fight. But, when due to weakness, his hands came down Israel was losing the fight. But, Aaron and Hur, who were Moses assistants, observing what was happening to their leader, held up his hands and put a stone under him which he sat upon. Thus Moses hands remained steady throughout the battle, resulting in the defeat of Amalek.

But Moses hands were heavy; and they took a stone and put it under him, and he sat there upon; and Aaron and Hur stayed up his hands, the one on the one side, and the other on the other side; and his hands were steady until the going down of the sun and Joshua discomfited Amalek and his people with the edge of the sword (Exod.17:12-13; cp. verses 8-16)

Only such a team effort can lead to a collective victory. We need faithful and sensitive "Aarons" and "Hurs", who will "hold up our hands" in ministry and dedicated "Joshuas" who can be trusted to minister in sensitive positions, under our spiritual oversight.

2. Nehemiah and his Co-workers

Nehemiah's ministry was successful because he was blessed with faithful and committed team workers. Though he was the leader, with a divine mission, he needed a strong team of assistants to help him fulfil his vision. When he unfolded his vision and mission, the people responded positively, willingly and heartily.

Then said I unto them, Ye see the distress that we are in, how Jerusalem lieth waste, and the gates there of are burned with fire: come, and let us build up the wall of Jerusalem, that we be no more a reproach. Then I told them of the hand of my God which was good upon me; as also the king's words that he had spoken unto me. And they said, let us rise up and build. So they strengthened their hands for this work (Neh.2: 17-18 AV).

Nehemiah attributed the success of his mission to a team effort, "for the people had a mind to work" (Neh.4:6). When threatened by Sanballat and Tobiah, Nehemiah set his men in strategic positions. While some were building the wall, others were fully armed, keeping watch. The rulers stood solidly behind the workers, in cooperation with Nehemiah. They all worked as a team toward a common goal (See: Neh.4:7-23).

Ministry work is what we have "received" from the Lord (Acts 20:24); Col.4:17) or delegated into, through the leadership of the Church (2 Tim.2:2; cp. Acts 6:1-6; Exod.17:13-26). You can do ministry or "do the work of ministry" in various capacities, depending on.

a. Your calling {1 Cor.7:20-22; 2 Peter 1:10}.

b. Your gifting (Prov.18:16; Rom.12:6-8; 1 Cor.12:8-10, 27-31).

c. Your Level of anointing (1 Sam.16:1-13; Isa.10:27; Acts 10:38; Psalm 45:7; 89:20; 92:10; Heb.1:9).

d. Your level of consecration (2 Tim.2:20-21).

e. Your level of faith (Rom.12:6).

f. Your level of grace (rom.12:5-6; Eph.4:7).

g. Your level of maturity (not a novice—1 Tim.3:6 See Uriah in the forefront of the hottest battle in 2 Sam.12:14-21).

h. Your level of experience

i. The wisdom and leading of the leadership of your Church (See: Exod.18:13-26; 2 Tim.2:2)

j. Your personal "ability" (See: Matt. 25:14-15).

k. Your level of spiritual understanding.

l. Your level of consecration

m. Your level of faithfulness.

n. Your level of wisdom.

There are different areas of ministry in the local Church. Such as:

a. Ministering in songs / music (1 Sam.16:23; 18:16; 1 Kings 4:32)[1]

b. Ministry of prayer (See: Col.4:32)

c. Ministering in counselling (Exod.18:13-25)

d. Ministry of the word (Acts 6:4)

e. Ministry of deliverance (Acts 3:1-9; 16:16-18, etc).

f. Ministering as an usher (2 Kings 25:18; 1 Chro.15:23, 24; Psa.4:10; John 18:16, 17).

g. Ministry of hospitality (Rom.12:13; 1 Tim.3:2; Tit.1:8; 1 Pet.4:9; See: The Shunmite woman—2 Kings 4).

h. Ministry of showing mercy (Rom.12:8—like the Good Samaritan)

i. Visitation ministry {Matt.25:36, 43; Acts 15:36; James 1:27}

j. Ministering in giving (Rom.12:8 cp.2 Cor.9:7; See: Ezra 2:69)

k. Ministry of helps (Greek: ANTILEPSIS—relief, help—1 Cor.12:28; See: Acts 11:29-30).

l. Ministry of praise worship {Acts 16:25; Heb.13:15 cp. 2 Chron. 5:13-14; 20:19-22}

m. Ministering to the various groups of people in the Church—the elderly, youth, children, families and singles.

n. Ministry dedicated to Church finances

o. Ministry of welfare {See: Acts 6:1; 9:36-39 etc.}

p. Ministry in charge of Church building {Exod.31:1-7; 35:30-35}

We also have the fivefold ministries

a. Apostolic ministry (Eph.4:11)

---

1 Chro.9:33; 15:12-27; 25:6, 7; 2 Chro.5:11-14; 7:6-7; 20:21; 23:13; 29:28; 34:12; 35:15; Eph.5:19; Col.3:16)

b. Prophetic ministry (Eph.4:11).

c. Evangelistic ministry (Eph.4:11)

d. Pastoral ministry (Eph.4:11)

e. Teaching ministry (Eph.4:11).

Examples of Bad Ministers

1. **Gehazi**—Elisha's servant (2 Kings 5:1-27)

Gehazi's example clearly demonstrates that being close to a prophet or leader does not automatically make one a potential leader. Gehazi had served well in relation to the Shunamites (in 2 Kings 4:11-31). But his weaknesses were revealed in his dealing with Naaman.

a. He was covetous (2 Kings 5:20, 21).

b. He was deceptive (verse 22).

c. He had a lying spirit: he lied to Naaman about his leader (verse 22) and he lied to his leader (verse 25).

d. He was unfaithful to his leader

e. He misrepresented the Church

f. He misrepresented his leader.

g. He had a hidden agenda.

h. He was a selfish / self-seeking worker.

i. He had no moral or personal integrity.

j. He secretly assigned to himself an illegitimate mission which was contrary to his leaders, vision and principles (verses 15-21, 26).

Consequently: Gehazi was exposed, humiliated and cursed with the leprosy of Naaman. The leprosy therefore of Naaman shall cleave unto thee, and unto thy seed forever. And he went out from his presence a leper as white as snow (2 Kings 5:27 AV)

The Ten Spies sent by Moses (Num.13:1-33)

Moses sent twelve ministers to view the Promised Land, in preparation of Israel towards their possession of the Land (See: Num.13:17-20). Ten of the ministers returned with negative and discouraging reports, which weakened the faith of the Church (See: Num.13:26-29, 31-33; cp. Num.14:7-10).

The ten ministers failed because:

a. They were fearful and timid

b. They were doubting and unbelieving

c. They walked by sight and not by faith.

d. They confessed negativities

e. They lacked the self confidence

f. They lacked sense of mission

g. They maximized their enemies and minimized God and His Church

h. They misrepresent God.

i. They misrepresented and disappointed their leader.

j. They misrepresented Israel / Church.

King Saul

Saul, King of Israel, is another bad example of a minister.

Instead of totally obeying his leader, Saul disobeyed Samuel and went to carry out his own personal agenda (1 Sam.15:4-31). Saul's unfaithful mission can be summed up as follows:

a. Partial obedience (verses 6-9) or total disobedience (verses 11, 19).

b. Selfish interest

c. Hidden agenda

d. Covetousness (verse 9)

e. Dishonesty

f. Half-heartedness (verse 20)

g. False righteousness (verse 13)

h. Zeal without wisdom and knowledge

i. Inability to fully understand and carryout the leader's vision

j. Inability to follow his leader's instruction

k. The spirit of formalism; having only a form of Godliness.

l. The spirit of rebellion (verse 23)

m. The spirit of stubbornness (verse 23)

n. Fear of man (verse 24)

o. Eye service / man pleasing spirit (verse 24; cp. 1 Sam.13:11, 12)

p. Lack of grace to remain humble after promoted (verses 17-19)

q. Sanctimonious, spirit making an outward show of holiness, but inwardly empty (verses 15, 21).

r. Saul had a bad habit of giving excuses and blaming other people, instead of taking responsibility for his sin (verses 15, 21; cp. 1Sam.13:11, 12).

s. Backslidden spirit (verse 11)

Qualities of a Good Minister

a. Faithfulness (Luke 12:42; 1 Cor.4:2).

b. Wisdom (Luke 12:42; 16:8)

c. Accountability and responsibility (Luke 12:42; 16:2)

d. Good (character, behaviour, attitudes)—Matt.25:21, 23; Luke 19:17)

e. Commitment and consistency (Luke 12:43)

f. Diligence (Matt.25:23)

g. Humility in service (Matt. 25:23)

h. Joy in service (Matt. 25:23)

i. Profitable and effectiveness (matt.25:17)

j. Good testimony / report (Luke 19:2)

k. Obedience to leadership (Luke 12:43; Matt. 25:16)

l. Blameless—above board, integrity {1 Tim.3:1-2}

m. The fear of God

n. Trustworthiness (Luke 12:42)

o. Ability to handle success (Matt. 25:21-23).

Qualities of a Bad Minister

a. Unfaithfulness (Matt.25:18, 24; Luke 12:45)

b. Unbelief and faithlessness

c. Spitefulness (Matt. 25:18, 26; Luke 19:20)

d. Murmuring, complaining and grumbling spirit (Matt. 25:24)

e. Wicked spirit (Matt. 25:26; Luke 19:22)

f. Unprofitable (Matt. 25:30)

g. Time serving attitudes (Luke 12:45)

h. Negligence of duty (Matt.25:18, 27)

i. Servile fear (Matt. 25:25)

j. Faintheartedness (Matt.25:24)

k. Lack of conscience (Matt. 25:18)

l. Unjust in service (Luke 16:8)

m. Disobedient spirit

n. Mediocre spirit

o. Stubborn and rebellious

p. Fault finding spirit (Matt.25:24)

q. Double minded (Luke 16:13)

r. Irresponsible spirit

s. Lack of accountability

Some Dangers to Avoid as Church Workers

There are some vices which Church workers are susceptible to. These vices can destroy you, ruin your usefulness and relationship with God. If not properly handled, they can destroy the whole Church. Therefore, you must resist them vigorously and guide against them prayerfully and religiously.

Envy and Jealousy

This is one of the most dangerous vices you must avoid as a Church worker.

    a. A worker can envy his / her leader.

There have been cases of Church workers who are envious or jealous of the position or blessings or success of their leaders. Such people do not normally see anything good in what their leader is doing. They are unduly critical, falsely accuse and negative towards their leaders. In some cases, they tend to influence other workers against their leaders. This was the case of Korah and his supporters against Moses.

Bible says: And they gathered themselves together against Aaron, and said unto them, ye take too much upon you, seeing all the congregation are holy, every one of them and the LORD is among them: wherefore then lift up ye up yourselves among the congregation of the LORD (Num.16:3; See also: Num.16:1-35; cp. Jude 11-12)

    b. It is common among Church workers to envy and be jealous of one another—especially where a worker is more effective, more anointed, more gifted or more favoured. Examples include:

        i. Cain was envious and jealous of Abel's success (Gen.4:4-5; See verses 1-11).

        ii. Joseph's brethren were jealous of him because he was favoured by their father (Gen.37:3-11; note verses 3-4).

        iii. Daniel's fellow workers envied his success and integrity (Dan.6:4; See verses 1-28)

        iv. The first set of labourers in the Lord's vineyard were jealous of the reward of the latter labourers (Matt.20:11-12; See verses 1-16).

        v. The elder brother of the prodigal son (Luke 15:28).

        vi. The unbelieving Jews were envious when the Gentiles received the gospel (Acts 13:45; See: verses 42-52).

        vii. David seemed to be envious of the prosperity of others. He confessed, "For I was envious of the foolish, when I saw the prosperity of the wicked" (Psalm 73:3).

viii. It is also possible for a leader to be envious or jealous of his / her subordinate. A leader may be jealous when a subordinate is more accepted, more successful, more gifted or anointed or more effective than the leader him selves. Examples include:

ix. King Saul started envying David when the congregation started ascribing more honour to David (1 Sam.18:9). But "David behaved himself wisely in all his ways" (1 Sam.18:5, 14, 15, 30; Psalm 101:2). Saul tried many times to kill David, but the Lord was on David's side (See: 1 Sam.18:10-30).

x. Haman was obviously envious of the popularity of Mordecai (See: Esther 5:13; See also: 3:1-15; contrast with 6:1-14).

Do not associate yourself with those who are envious or jealous of their leaders. If you sense any seed of envy or jealousy in your heart, pray against it and root it out. Envy can destroy you, as it has destroyed others.

Qualifications for Ministry Workers

Church work or ministry is not a secular or a worldly work, it is a sacred or spiritual work. Therefore, everyone who is called to serve in the Church must be spiritually and morally qualified to serve. Every Church worker or minister must possess the following basic qualifications.

1. A regenerated life (John 3:1-7).
2. A consecrated or surrendered life
3. A Spirit filled life
4. Spiritual maturity (not a novice—1 Tim.3:6)
5. A habitual life of prayer
6. Knowledge of the Bible
7. Personal integrity
8. A teachable spirit / willingness to learn
9. A life governed by wisdom
10. A life governed by the fear of God
11. A humble spirit or a servant spirit.

A consecrated life

Consecration simply means "to be set apart" unto God and His work. As a Church worker, you must be totally consecrated to Christ and His service. You must be set apart or separated from questionable things, people and habits, for sacred use. Another word for consecration is the surrendered life. You must surrender or set apart to God:

1. Your Body (Rom.12:1-2)

2. Your Time {Eph.5:16; Col.4:5}

3. Your personal pleasure

4. Your money

5. Your entire being (1 Thes.5:23)

A consecrated life is characterized by a crucified life, rendering selfless service, total commitment or submission to the will of God. Jesus reflected this submissive spirit; He said: "Not as I will, but as thou wilt" {Matt.26:39; See also: Job 1:21; Mark 14:36 etc.}. John the Baptist reflected this attitude when he said, in relation to Jesus, "He must increase, but I must decrease" {John 3:30}. This submissive spirit can also be reflected in the following ways:

a. A life governed by the fear of God.

b. A life governed by humility

c. A life governed by holiness

d. A consistent life of prayer and devotion to the Word of God.

e. Willingness to serve

f. A wholehearted attitude to the service of God.

The Importance of Consecrated Life

a. The Word of God demands it

b. God uses only consecrated Christians

c. Consecration is necessary for success in ministry

d. Consecration is necessary for your personal blessing / wellbeing

e. Anointing is released through consecration

1. 1 Chro.9:33; 15:12-27; 25:6, 7; 2 Chro.5:11-14; 7:6-7; 20:21; 23:13; 29:28; 34:12; 35:15; Eph.5:19; Col.3:16)

Contributor

The Practical Policy Making and Job Description in Christian Ministry and Mission is a treasure trove of leadership insight and information for the 21st century church. Being a book able to cover the fundamental concepts for preparation and guidance for church leadership, it becomes the focal point and reference in empowering successful church leaders. This book will expand on the experience of ministry, and further foresee the ministry beyond mission and planning. This work fits within the concepts of policy, procedures, implementation and execution of the same.

The work dives into the concept to empower leaders with a mind-set for sustainability of the church. The flow of information focuses on experiences to establish a model within the experiences of ministry. It becomes the guide to prepare beyond pastoral care, preaching and teaching. As a directive in the use of this book; the audience in mind is the person who is already in a place of church leadership or who is anticipating a leadership responsibility. One will find an expository understanding in ministry through these chapters.

Biblical foundation is essential to this book. It offers an understanding of the practice of leadership from the unique perspective impacting leadership development. As sustainability is the greatest challenge in leadership development, leaders who are genuinely interested in making great leaders will enhance these chapters for effectiveness. I can agree that the twenty-first century Church leadership must respond to its challenges, just like business must respond to its competitive world. Enhance your ministry through the vision of the author, as his foresight is for a standard of excellence in Ministry. This book will impact leadership success.

Deloris C. Henry, B.A, M. M., D. M.,

Consultant in Leadership Development

Pastor in the New Calvary Life Ministries, USA

Chapter Three

The Ministry of an Apostle

The word Apostle, from the Greek "Apostolos", means one sent forth. An Apostle, then is one sent forth with a "Divine Commission". More than the act of sending, this word includes the idea of the authorization of a messenger. The word "apostle" is exclusively a New Testament term. However, it conveys the idea of commissioning and empowering of the prophets called and sent by God in the Old Testament {See: Exod.3:10; Isa.6:8; Jer. 1:7). In the New Testament apostle is applied to Jesus as the Sent One of God {Hebrew 3:1}, to those sent by God to preach to Israel {Luke 11:49}, to those sent by churches {2 Cor.8:23; Phil.2:25}, and most often, to the individuals who had been appointed by Christ to preach the gospel of the kingdom. The twelve disciples chosen by the Lord for special training were called apostles {Luke 6:13; 9:10}.

Having direct knowledge of the incarnate Word, and being sent out as authorized agents of the gospel, the apostles provided the authentic interpretation of the life and teaching of Jesus Christ. They were regarded as the "pillars of the Church" and the foundation of the church, and their teaching became the norm for Christian Faith and practice. The mystery of Divine truths was revealed to and transmitted through the apostles {Eph.3:5}, the pillars of the Church.

Paul wrote: And when James, Cephas, and John, who seemed to be pillars, perceived the grace that was given unto me, they gave to me and Barnabas the right hands of fellowship; that we should go unto the heathen, and they unto the circumcision {Galatians 2:9 AV}.

Again he wrote, to the church:

Now therefore ye are no more strangers and foreigners, but fellow citizens with the saints, and of the household of God; and are built upon the foundation of the apostles and prophets, Jesus Christ himself being the chief corner stone; in whom all the building fitly framed together growth unto a holy temple in the lord; in whom ye also are builded together for a habitation of God through the Spirit {Ephesians 2:19-22 AV}.

While John wrote: And the wall of the city had twelve foundations, and in them the names of the twelve apostles of the Lamb {Revelation 21: 14 AV}.

It is evident that the apostles formed the nucleus of primitive Christianity. The New Testament highlights their function as apostles, without delineating in detail the authoritative nature of their office in relation to the church, as one that is a 'foundation layer'.—1 Corn 3:10. These apostles are responsible for policy making, strategy, direction, economic development in the church, whether local, national or international. The level of authority of an apostle depends on the number of churches and the areas covered by his spiritual leadership. Paul, for example, was the apostle of the Gentile churches, while Peter was the apostle of the Jewish churches.

There were obviously some "false apostles and deceitful workers" who made themselves apostles {2 Cor. 11:13}. We have men and women who call themselves apostles, but not by God {See: Rev.2:2}.

We have to be very careful not to get trapped into following the wrong kinds of leadership of men and women who are making or assuming themselves apostles but are not. An apostle is not just someone who travels. An apostle is a forerunner, one who goes before. He is one that pioneers. He is one who brings vision, strategy, direction, government, structure, correction, order and life. He brings spirituality where there was none. He or she brings revelation, deliverance, healing, removing demonic spirits, releasing captives. He or she unfolds mysteries. He or she brings the times to their fullness. He or she knows KAIROS moments. He or she understands regular and current rhema words. He or she walks in a new realm of authority. He or she leads people into their spiritual promised land, and this I did when I started this ministry namely: Mount Calvary Church in Feb. 2011

And are built upon the foundation of the apostles and prophets, Jesus Christ himself being the chief corner stone; in whom all the building fitly framed together growth unto an Holy Temple in the Lord: In whom ye also are builded together for an habitation of God through the Spirit (Ephesians 2:20-22 AV).

What marks do we look for in an Apostle today?

1. The outstanding spiritual gifts that is released from apostolic mantle as an umbrella over a region—local, national and international—where others benefit from the thrust of his anointing. When the wave of the Spirit and the anointing of God hit that region it brings protection for growth, maturity, accountability and release.

2. A deep personal experience with God, a clear Word, a now Word, or a moment word. Like the word of Gideon, the word of Joshua, and the word of David, God is still giving His clear, specific and timely Word to His Church through His chosen apostles today. As one of God's chosen vessels with an apostolic calling and unction, I have found this experience to be a reality in my ministry. That clear word will become the very foundational force that brings a clear revelation which eventually brings destruction to the enemies hold in that city and places where God is using His apostle. The Word spoken by God's apostle will convey miraculous blessings. The Bible says, "He sent forth his Word and it healeth them" {Psa.107:20}. The churches—local, national or international—will usually benefit for the apostolic mandate of their leader. Thus, they will be positively and profoundly motivated to mobilize themselves alongside the word, and bring a corporate blessing to their city and to their ministry.

3. The voice of the apostle speaks with unction and power. It is like a trumpet in the heavenlies over regions. An apostle lifts up his "voice like a trumpet" {Isa.58:1} and declares God's Word, with the "demonstration of the Spirit and power" {1 Cor.2:4} in the realms or provinces covered by his apostolate. His voice causes spiritual forces to be mobilized—in the heavenly and earthly realms—to unite and demolish demonic assignments in those realms. Moreover, by reason of this apostolic unction and empowerment, more churches are planted, existing churches are strengthened and powered and

men and women are released with unction to function in various ministries within and outside those realms.

4. Ability to provide adequate spiritual leadership with correction, vision and direction. It has to do with authority and anointing. Also it brings certain reassignments, readjustments, righteousness, and moral rule to churches and ministries, local, national and international. This also speaks of bestowing authority of rulership that is placed to govern. It is also known has the apostolic seat, where they have a strong influence of authority bestowed on them, that their voice is honoured and respected in the governmental ream. In Acts 1, we find that Matthias was placed into the apostle's seat instead of Judas. Also in Acts 15, James sits and rules.

5. An apostle should be one that has the power to preach the gospel with signs and wonders. Paul defended his apostleship, when he said: Truly the signs of an apostle were wrought among you in all patience, in signs, and wonders, and mighty deeds (2 Corinthians 12:12 AV). See also: Acts 11v21-26; 13v50; 14v19-23). He should also be committed to establishing Churches and other leadership in the works of the Kingdom. The apostles of the early church were committed to church planting and training leaders to oversee local assemblies. Paul travelled extensively and established several churches. To the Corinthians, he said, I have planted, Apollos watered; but God gave the increase" {1 Cor.3:6}. Again, he said, "as a wise master builder, I have laid the foundation, and another buildeth there upon" {1 Cor.3:10}.

6. An Apostle is committed to the point of risking his life for the sake of the name of Christ and the gospel.

Paul said: But none of these things move me, neither count I my life dear unto myself, so that I might finish my course with joy, and the ministry, which I have received of the LORD Jesus, to testify the gospel of the grace of God {Acts 20:24AV}.

Again, he said, "For me to live is Christ, and to die is gain" {Phil.1:21}.

An Apostle may be able to function as a Prophet, Teacher, Evangelist and Pastor. He is the combination of all the four. Not all apostles are equal in ministry and responsibilities. They differ in the anointing, power, and the nature of their ministries. Some have lesser spiritual power and authority.

For example, we have over twenty-five apostles mentioned in the New Testament but we only hear of a few who moved in such great anointing as Paul, Peter, and Barnabas.

Two Categories of Apostles

The Twelve Apostles of the Lamb (Rev. 21:14; Matt. 10:2-4)

They were the twelve who walked with Jesus. They are the foundational apostles: namely, Peter, James, John, Andrew, Philip, Thomas, Bartholomew, Matthew, James, the son of Alphaeus, Simon the Zealot, Judas, son of James, and Matthias.

They were the original disciples who witnessed the ministry, life, death, resurrection, and Ascension of our Lord. Though the original apostles died, the office of an apostle still exists. Our Lord is sending out apostles across the nations to establish His work. The Church today must continue to build on the foundation established by the first apostles. We must obey and remain faithful to their teachings. To reject their teachings in any way is to stray from the biblical pattern of Christianity (John 16:13-15; 1Cor. 14: 36-38; Gal.1: 9-11).

The Apostles of the Ascended Christ

They are those who are called and set in the Body to hold the "office" of apostleship, the same way a Prophet, an Evangelist, a Pastor or a Teacher is called today.

The ones listed in the New Testament are:

a. Matthias—Acts 1:23-26

b. Barnabas—Acts 14:14

c. Paul—Acts 14:14; 1 Cor.1:1

d. James—the Lord's brother—Acts 1:14; 1 Cor.15:7; Gal.1:19

e. Timothy—1 Thess.1:1; 1 Tim.1:2; 5:22

f. Andronicus—Rom. 16:7.

g. Apollo's—Acts 4:36. 1Cor. 4: 6-9; 9: 6.

h. Junias—Rom. 16:7.

i. Epaphroditus—Phil. 2:25

j. Judas—Acts 15:22.

k. Silas—Acts 15:22; 1Thes. 1:1; 2 Cor. 8:2; Titus 1:4

Work of an Apostle

As I have earlier stated, the name "Apostle" means the sent one. However, it should be noted that not all Apostles are pioneers (1Cor. 9:1). It should also be noted that the primary task of the New Testament apostles was to establish new Churches and ensure that they were laid on strong foundations. They made sure that these Churches maintained the purity of faith and they strongly defended the gospel against heresy and false teachings see (Rom. 16: 17; 1Cor. 5: 1-5; 11: 2; 2Cor. 6:14-18; James 2:14-26 and etc).

Again, Paul said: Yea, so have I strived to preach the gospel, not where Christ was named, lest I should build upon another man's foundation (Roman 15: 20 AV).

An apostle travels to different churches of his circuit to establish or set them in good order.

The scope of his apostleship is limited to the Churches he has established or those that are under his care. Let us assume that Paul was not accepted as an apostle by every Church. His work was limited to the scope of ministry to which God called him. He ministered more to the Gentiles than to the Jews. We should also note that Paul never exercised authority or oversight over Churches that other Apostles established. This meant that an apostle should not expect his ministry to be accepted by all.

Paul wrote to the Christians in Corinth:

Am I not free? Am I not an apostle? Have I not seen Jesus our Lord? Are you not the result of my work in the Lord? Even though I may not be an apostle to others, surely I am to you! For you are the seal of my apostleship in the Lord (1Corinthians 9:1-2 AV).

An apostle's work is to build the Body of Christ, by revealing the "Revelation of Christ". He gives importation to establish a strong foundation in the Body (Col. 2: 2; Rom.1: 11). An apostle helps in setting things in order where there is chaos (1 Cor.11:34). But again, it has to be within his particular scope of ministry. For example, in Mount Calvary Holy Church of America International, the Bishop Brumfield Johnson was used by God as an apostle to establish a vision and to build the hearts of leaders. The church has to be established and set in the right order according to the blueprint or the pattern given by the Holy Spirit.

This can be initiated by the leading Bishop in a church. An apostle can also be involved in ordaining and appointing other ministries. For example, Paul and Barnabas ordained elders by the laying on of hands with prayer and fasting in the churches they established (Acts 14:13). Paul was also involved in the presbytery and impartation of spiritual gifts in the ordination of Timothy to the ministry. This was the case in my ministry, when my former leader Bishop Harold I. Williams imparted some spiritual gifts to me during my ordination in August11, 1995 to the Pastoral Ministry. Moreover, he said that when he returned he would give me further directions. This was the Bible reading:

I left you in Crete, so that you could put in order the things that still needed doing and appoint church elders in every town. Remember my instructions: (Titus 1: 5 GNV). The following Scriptures were also read, during my ordination: Acts 14: 23; Rom. 1:11; 1Cor. 3:10-11; 1 Tim. 1:18; 4:14; 5: 22, 2 Tim. 1:6.)

An apostle has a vision for the entire Body of Christ. His vision is not limited to a single group of people. Also, an apostle and a prophet can work together to impart a vision or insight to the Church body. The local Church has to be made aware of the plans and the purposes of God World-Wide. The Prophet and Apostle have an eye to see more broadly and can help establish the local Church in the proper functions within the wider framework. This will help the church to understand more fully the purposes and the plans of God for them according to Acts 14: 21-23, 15:6-21.

An apostle can be used of God to root out or pull down an establishment that is out of order (Jer.1:10). He can also be used to restore discipline in the local Church or ministry under his supervision. A key note—Peter condemned Ananias and Sapphira for falsehood (Acts 5:1-11).—Paul instructed the Corinthian Church on how to deal with sin in their midst (1Cor. 4:21; 5:1-13; 2Cor. 2:6-11; 13:2, 10). Pointing out and correcting falsehoods can be a very painful process. See also: 1Cor. 4: 14-15; 2Cor. 12: 14; 15; 1Thes. 2: 5-12)

Today Apostle Works

This has to do with the apostles insight into the things of God. It has to do with his ability to discern in the spirit realm and be able to distinguish the heavenlies from the natural. In this Scripture of (2 Corinthians 10:13AV), Paul began to speak about the authenticity of his ministry and his calling as an apostle. He said:

But we will not boast of things without our measure, but according to the measure of the rule which God hath distributed to us, a measure to reach even unto you {2 Corinthians 10:13AV}.

This Scripture shows two things, spheres of influence and measures of rule. I like to look at this in three areas {local, national and international}.

Local Apostle: The local apostle that comes to a community to start a church might not necessarily be an apostle to the national or international ministry. He might be called as an apostle over the terrain of his establishment. There are other apostles whose sphere of operation may be within local, national and sometimes international. We also need to note that not everyone who plants churches is an apostle; that is, not everyone who plants a church has an apostolic calling. An Evangelist or a lay minister can plant a church. The church in Antioch, for example, was not planted by an apostle, but by lay Christians, who "went everywhere preaching the Word" (Acts 8:4; See also: Acts 11:19). Today, most of the ministers who plant churches are called "missionaries". The rank and calling of an apostle is given by Christ Jesus as He wills. It is a local sphere and God is the only one who can determine the boundaries by which that measure is given. It is in that dominion or sphere that the individual has authority and leadership and power over demonic spirits.

National Apostle: This apostle is given to a nation to speak words that are pertinent to that nation at any given moment. They have the ability to see all of the things pertaining to the nation in terms of strategy and where the nation is going. The national apostle and the local apostle can work together to bring healing, revival and reformation to the nation

International Apostle: These apostles are given to a continent. The mandate of these apostolic men and women is determined by the measure of rule and authority that God has given them. Sometimes they are called chief apostles. The amount of revelation that an individual is given determines their depth of authority. Every revelation has an amount of light that is released. Each apostle can use his apostolic mandate to form a council where on individual has a vote or speak on issues they can actually determine the move, the thrust, the trends, and the spiritual movements of a nation because of the seat of the apostolic council in the heavenlies. When local, national and international apostles work together, an irresistible power is released which can destroy the assignments of territorial demons in that continent.

Contributor

The author of this book: "Practical Policy Making and Job Description in Christian Ministry and Mission" have been known to me as Bishop Allan Miller for the past eighteen months as a credible, God fearing servant of God whose passion is to see the work of the ministry advancing, by first applying the Early Apostolic Biblical Principles and secondly by applying some of our 21st Century technological principles to run an effective church.

The book is a manual for ministry and it has appeared at such a time as this, when it seems the church does not know what it is doing, with regards to the fivefold ministry, the need to acknowledge the use of other gifts in running the church and the need for proper financial accountability. Bishop Allan sets out financial principles to help the Minister to avoid the mismanagement of the finances of the church. There is a clear indication that the minister cannot do ministry alone, therefore, it is imperative to rely on other gifts that would enhance the building of a successful and a healthy church. Bishop Allan goes on to explain each function of the five-fold ministry and the subsidiary ministries that projects a healthy church.

The book acts as a guidebook for both Pastors and ministers in churches of all sizes and locations. The book reveals most of the practicalities of ministry. There are many things a minister learns along the road in caring for the flock of the Lord. Sometimes the knowledge comes by hard experience but here is a book to eliminate some of the hard experiences with regards to running a church. The book would help to liberate the wondering minds of ministers in ministry and for those who are aspiring to be in ministry. There is a whole world to win, we must do our assignment well and with perfection.

The book sets out some instructive and key fundamental insight necessary to establish a church in the 21st Century, incorporating the old apostolic order with our new technological order for a progressive church. I would recommend this book to every minister who wants to do ministry well to the glory of the Lord.

Grace C Sackie-Osae, BA. MA., PhD.

Host Minister of the Croydon Branch: Amazing Grace Ministries (KC)

Bishop of Amazing Grace Ministries (KC)

Chapter Four

The Ministry of a Prophet

A prophet was an individual who received a call from God to be God's spoke person, often connected with some crisis that was about to occur, and then announced God's message of judgment and / or deliverance to a person, or people or the nations. The importance of this office can be seen in the fact that the word "prophet" occurs in the Old and New Testament. The only safe course in resolving the meaning of a word is to depend ultimately on usages in contexts.

Basically, a prophet is a person who speaks on behalf of God. In the Old Testament, the Hebrew noun "nabi" is used for "prophet". Old Testament prophets were God's mouthpieces, as we can in {Exod.7:1; 1 Chron.29:29}. This basic meaning finds support in other passages, such as {Deut.18:14-22}.

In the New Testament, the Greek word used is "prophetes", a proclaimer of Divine message or one who speaks on behalf of God. It was used among the Greeks to denote an interpreter of the oracles of the gods. But God's anointed prophet is an interpreter of God's oracle, who speaks as the "oracle of God" {cp. 1 Peter 4:11}.

However, in spite of the absence of any or all definitive consensus on the real meaning of the word "prophet" there are at least two classical texts that demonstrate the usage of this term and its meaning in the biblical texts. The first is Exodus.

And the Lord said unto Moses, see, I have made thee a god to Pharaoh: and Aaron thy brother shall be thy prophet. Thus shalt speak all that I command thee: and Aaron thy brother shall speak unto Pharaoh that he send the children of Israel out of his land {Exodus 7:1-2 AV}.

Moreover, a prophet is authorized to communicate this Divine message to another. Thus Aaron was to function as Moses' mouthpiece.

And thou shalt speak unto him, and put words in his mouth: and I will be with thy mouth, and with his mouth, and will teach you what ye shall do. And he shall be thy spokesman unto the people: and he shall be, even he shall be to thee instead of a mouth, and thou shalt be to him instead of God {Exodus 4:15-16 AV}.

The second classical texts is Numbers chapter twelve.

And he said, hear now my words: If there be a prophet among you, I the Lord will make myself known unto him in a vision, and will speak unto him in dream. My servant Moses is not so, who is faithful in all mine house. With him will I speak mouth to mouth, even apparently, and not in dark speeches; and the similitude of the Lord shall he behold: wherefore then were ye not afraid to speak against my servant Moses? {Numbers 12:6-8 AV}.

Clearly, then, a prophet was an authorized spokesperson for God with a message that originated with God and was communicated through a number of means. When God spoke to these spokespersons, they had no choice but to deliver that word to those to whom God directed it. When a true prophet speaks, he speaks with "Divine Inspiration and Revelation". He does not fabricate or speak things on his own. He speaks what the Holy Spirit gives him. This prophet can communicate or declare God's thoughts to the people. These thoughts could have the purpose of warning, reproving, edifying, bringing comfort or exhortation. The prophet is the spokesman for God. He speaks with authority because of the anointing and the hand of the Lord upon his life.

The Calling and Qualifications of a Prophet

The calling of a prophet is crucial, and he must know for sure that he has been called to this Ministry. He must have an inner conviction. It is impossible to demonstrate from the texts of Scripture that each person called to be a prophet received a specific call from God; however, that fact may be explained by the brevity of our study. It is true, nevertheless, that there were many who "prophesied" who were not called to be prophets, but were called to be judges, leaders, or priests. Thus, Gideon delivered Israel from the hand of the Midianites, acting on rather detailed instructions from the Lord as to how he was to effect such a deliverance, much as a true prophet would receive revelation from God.

And the Lord said unto Gideon, the people that are with thee are too many for me to give the Midianites into their hands, lest Israel vaunt themselves against me saying, mine own hand hath saved me. And the Lord said unto Gideon, the people are yet too many; bring them down unto the water, and I will try them for thee there: and it shall be, that of whom I say unto thee, this shall go with thee, the same shall go with thee; and of whomsoever I say unto thee, this shall not go with thee, the same shall not go. And the Lord said unto Gideon, by the three hundred men that lapped will I save you, and deliver the Midianites into thine hand: and let all the other people go every man unto his place {Judges 7:2, 4, 7 AV}.

The official institution of the office of a prophet took place in Moses' day.

The LORD thy God will raise up unto thee a Prophet from the midst of thee, of thy brethren, like unto me; unto him ye shall hearken; according to all that thou desirest of the LORD thy God in Horeb in the day of the assembly, saying, let me not hear again the voice of the LORD neither let me see this great fire any more, that I die not. And the LORD said unto me, they have well spoken that which they have spoken. I will raise them up a Prophet from among their brethren, like unto thee, and will put my words in his mouth; and he shall speak unto them all that that I shall command him. And it shall come to pass, that whosoever will not hearken unto my words which he shall speak in my name, I will require it of him. But the prophet, which shall presume to speak a word in my name, which I have not commanded him to speak, or that shall speak in the name of other gods, even that prophet shall die. And if thou say in thine heart, how shall we know the word which the LORD hath not spoken? When a prophet speaketh in the name of the LORD, if the thing follow not, nor come to pass, that is the thing which the LORD hath not spoken, but the prophet hath spoken it presumptuously: thou shalt not be afraid of him {Deuteronomy 18:15-22 AV}.

A prophet is never appointed by men, but by the Holy Spirit. God does the choosing by divine appointment and confirms the ministries with an anointing of power. One does not become a prophet by working or studying hard. He is made by God and empowered by the Holy Spirit. A prophet must be capable of hearing the voice of God and be able to convey it to the people.

He must be a man of character and spiritual understanding, according to Titus 1v8-9.

But a lover of hospitality, a lover of good men, sober, just, holy, temperate; Holding fast the faithful word as he hath been taught, that he may be able by sound doctrine both to exhort and to convince the gainsayers (Titus 1:8-9AV).

Misconceptions of Prophetic Ministry:

Many think prophets do know everything about everybody and everything that is happening around them. Nathan had said to David, "Go, do all that is in thine heart; for the LORD is with thee" {2 Sam.7:3}. But it was not God's will for David to build a house for God; Solomon, his son, would build it instead. The story of Shunammite's son—the Lord hath hid it from me, and hath not told me.10 (See: 2 Kings 4:18-37).

Also the story of Simon the Sorcerer—offered the apostles money (Acts 8:1-24). Oftentimes a prophet knew only a portion of the Divine will. For example, Samuel knew that he was to anoint one of Jesse's sons, but he did not know which one (1 Samuel 16). His guess was that it would be one of the older sons, but it was only after David, Jesse's youngest son, stood before him that he knew that he had been looking at external appearances while God looked on the heart of the one who was to be anointed as king.

Prophets of the Bible

Old Testament Prophets

How did God communicate His Word to His prophets? In rare cases, God spoke in an audible voice that could be heard by anyone who might have been in the vicinity. Such was Samuel's experience when he heard his name being called out in the middle of the night (1 Samuel 3:3-9).

And ere the lamp of God went out in the temple of the Lord, where the ark of God was, and Samuel was laid down to sleep; that the Lord called Samuel: and he answered, here am I. and he ran unto Eli, and said, Here am I; for thou calledst me. And he said, I called not; lie down again. And he went and lay down. And the Lord called yet again, Samuel. And Samuel arose and went to Eli, and said, here am I; for thou didst call me. And he answered, I called not, my son; lie down again. Now Samuel did not yet know the Lord, neither was the word of the Lord yet revealed unto him. And the Lord called Samuel again the third time. And he arose and went to Eli, and said, here am I; for thou didst call me. And Eli perceived that the Lord had called the child. Therefore Eli said unto Samuel, go, lie down: and it shall be, if he call thee, that thou shalt say, speak Lord; for thy servant heareth. So Samuel went and lay down in his place (1 Samuel 3:3-9 AV).

Elijah would later come to this cave, where God would converse with his thoroughly disheartened servant (1 Kings 19:9-14).

And he came thither unto a cave, and lodged there; and, behold, the word of the Lord came to him, and he said unto him, what doest thou here, Elijah? And he said, I have been very jealous for the LORD God of hosts: for the children of Israel have forsaken thy covenant thrown down thine alters, and slain thy prophets with the sword; and I, even I only, am left; and they seek my life, to take it away. And he said, go forth, and stand upon the mount before the LORD. And, behold, the LORD passed by, and a great and strong wind rent the mountains, and brake in pieces the rocks before the LORD; but the LORD was not in the wind: and after the wind an earthquake; but the LORD was not in the earthquake: and after the earthquake a fire; but the LORD was not in the fire: and after the fire a still small voice. And it was so, when Elijah heard it, that he wrapped his face in his mantle, and went out, and stood in the entering in of the cave. And, behold, there came a voice unto him, and said, what doest thou here, Elijah? And he said, I have been very jealous for the LORD God of hosts: because the children of Israel have forsaken thy covenant, thrown down thine alters, and slain thy prophets with the sword; and I, even I only, am left; and they seek my life, to take it away. (1 Kings 19:9-14 AV).

More frequently, the prophet received a direct message from God with no audible voice. Instead, there must have been an internal voice by which the consciousness of the prophet suddenly was so heightened that he knew beyond a shadow of a doubt that what he said or what he was to do was exactly what God wanted done in that situation. So accurate was this type of communication by a man of God that Elisha did in (2 Kings 6:10-12 AV).

And the king of Israel sent to the place which the man of God told him and warned him of, and saved himself there, not once nor twice. Therefore, the heart of the king of Syria was sore troubled for this thing; and he called his servants, and said unto them, will ye not show me which of us is for the king of Israel? And one of his servants said, none, my lord, O king: but Elisha, the prophet that is in Israel, telleth the king of Israel the words that thou speakest in thy bedchamber (2 Kings 6:10-12 AV).

God also communicated with his prophets in a third way: by opening the prophet's eyes so that he could see realities that ordinarily would be hidden. Thus, just as the LORD opened the eyes of Balaam's donkey so that she saw what Balaam at first could not see (Number 22:31), so God opened the eyes of the prophet Elisha's servant so that he could see the angelic armies of the LORD that surrounded Samaria were indeed greater in number than the Syrian armies (2 Kings 6: 15-17 AV).

Then the LORD opened the eyes of Balaam, and he saw the angel of the LORD standing in the way, and his sword drawn in his hand: and he bowed down his head, and fell flat on his face (Numbers 22:31 AV).

And when the servant of the man of God was risen early, and gone forth, behold, a host compassed the city both with horses and chariots. And his servant said unto him, alas, my master! How shall we do? And he answered, fear not: for they that be with us are more than they that be with them. And Elisha prayed, and said, LORD, I pray thee, open his eyes, that he may see. And the LORD opened the eyes of the young man; and he saw: and behold, the mountain was full of horses and chariots of fire round about Elisha (2 Kings 6:15-17 AV).

The fourth way that God communicated with his prophets was the extensive use of visions, dreams, and elaborate imagery. God's word was sometimes clothed in symbolic imagery that left a firm imprint on the mind of the prophet and his listeners. For example, in the book of Daniel chapter two.

You, O king, are a king of kings: for the God of Heaven has given you a kingdom, power, and strength, and glory. And wheresoever the children of men dwell, the beasts of the field and the fowls of the heaven has He given into your hand, and has made you ruler over them all. You are this head of gold. And after you shall arise another kingdom inferior to you, and another third kingdom of brass, which shall bear rule over all the earth (Daniel 2:37-39 AV).

The visions God gave did not come at any special time. Some came while the prophet was awake; others came while the prophet was awakened from his sleep or was sleeping. In some cases the prophet was transported in a vision to places far distant from the place or locality where he was (Ezek 8:1-3; 11:24). Yet the prophet always retained the ability to distinguish between his own dreams and those that were given by God.

And it came to pass in the sixth year, in the sixth month, in the fifth day of the month, as I at in my house, and the elders of Judah sat before me, that the Hand of the lord God fell there upon me. Then I beheld, and lo a likeness as the appearance of fire: from the appearance of His loins even downward, fire; and from His loins even upward, as the appearance of brightness, as the colour of amber. And He put forth the form of an hand, and took me by a lock of my head; and the Spirit lifted me up between the Earth and the heaven, and brought me in the visions of God to Jerusalem, to the door of the inner gate that looks toward the north; where was the seat of the image of jealousy, which provokes to jealousy (Ezekiel 8:1-3 AV).

Afterwards the Spirit took me up, and brought me in a vision by the Spirit of God into Chaldea, to them of the captivity. So the vision that I had seen went up from me (Ezekiel 11:24 AV).

In order to understand the ministry and functions of a prophet today, we must first be able to understand the prophets of the Bible days. An Old Testament prophet was God's mouthpiece.

They were known as: Seers (1 Sam. 9:9; 2 Sam. 24:11), Man of God (1 Sam. 9:6), Servants (Hag. 2:3), Messengers (Mal. 3:1), Prophets (Hos.12:10; Matt. 10:31).

In the Old Testament, prophets such as Moses, Elisha, Samuel, Aaron and Elijah were used to give guidance to the people. People looked upon them for spiritual guidance and leadership. Other prophets such as Daniel and Zechariah were seers who saw the future through visions and dreams.

Prophets such as Ezekiel, Jeremiah, Isaiah, Joel, Hosea, and others were used not only to prophesy, but also to write the infallible Word of God.

New Testament Prophets

In the New Testament, believers are led by the Holy Spirit and God's Word, not by prophets or prophecies. God may use a prophet to confirm something He has already revealed to the believer.

The prophetic ministry is different from the gift of prophecy. The gift of prophecy can function in any Spirit—filled believer. However, this will not make him a prophet. All prophets must have the gift of prophecy functioning in their ministries, but all who operate in the gift of prophecy are not necessarily prophets. The office of a prophet operates in at least two or three revelation gifts consistently.

1. **Word of Wisdom**. The word "wisdom" is translated from the Greek "Sophia". The word is used in reference to 'an insight into the true nature of things'. Worldly wisdom depends on human knowledge and eloquence (1 Corn. 1:17, 20, 27; 2:1, 4, 5) but God's Wisdom is the revelation of the things which had once been secret and hidden, by the Holy Spirit, to God's people. See also: Gen. 41: 37-39; 2 Sam. 12: 1-14; 2Chrn. 1: 10-12; 1 Kings 3:9-12, 4:29-34).

2. **Word of Knowledge.** The word "knowledge" is translated from the Greek "Gnosis". The gift of the 'word of knowledge' gives us the ability to know, by the revelation of the Holy Spirit, the particular actions that had already taken place or presently taking place. It is a gift of spiritual perception. It is a very sensitive gift. The individual who possesses this gift conveys God's message to the Church; he speaks the truth desired by the Holy Spirit for a specific situation. (See Peter dealing with Ananias and Sapphira in Acts 5:1-10; Elisha was able to know that Gahazi had coveted after Naman gifts which Elisha had earlier rejected (2 Kings 5:20-26).

3. **Discerning of Spirit.** The Greek noun "Diakrisis" is the word used in (1 Corn. 12:10) for 'discerning', of "discern" spirits, judging by evidence whether they are evil or of God. The same word is used in 1 Corn. 11:29. It usually refers to "distinguishing between" or a

52

"judicial estimation". Its meaning also includes a clear discrimination of, to judge by evidence whether something is good or bad, acceptable or unacceptable, from the Biblical point of view. The discerning gift, is the only gift which is spiritually capable of this.12. See also: 2 Sam. 19: 35; 1 Kings 3: 9; Is. 11: 3; Ezek. 44: 23; Mal. 3: 18; Luke 12: 56; 1 Corn. 2: 14.

Contributor

D r Allan P. Miller has set out a clear mandate of not only: "Practical Policy Making and Job Description in Christian Ministry and Mission" but also how one should achieve and exercise such philosophy and theological call on their life. Work alongside Bishop Allan Miller for the past eighteen years as a credible, God fearing servant of God whose passion is to see the work of the ministry advancing, by first applying the Early Apostolic Biblical Principles and secondly by applying some of our 21st Century technological principles to run an effective church.

This book is profound and a scholarly call to the liberal Church leaders to return from the morass of theological relativism, to the sold ground of Christian Theology. A principle of authentic Christian leadership is that in order to be effective leaders, we must first become committed followers. In both the Old and New Testaments, effectual leaders possessed that common denominator of being followers of God. Jesus understood that fact. That, it seems to me, is the foundational step of authentic Christian leadership pointed out within each ministerial role by Rev Dr Allan P Miller.

In the Practical Policy Making and Job Description in Christian Ministry and Mission Dr Miller writes with equal clarity, as he shows that the Doctrine of Christian Ministry has been the only adequate response that the Church Mission has made to God's revelation of Himself in history. This book is written to provide a greater in-depth exposition of what it means, to experience the Pastoral Community and how you can fulfil your place in the call to minister the words of God that is so much needed in these desperate and dark days.

Dr. Miller's observations can never be any question about the educational acumen he brings to bear upon his subject, or the skill with which he pens his views. There is nothing more fundamental or necessary in today's World than education. I am convinced that this work will be of great benefit to the Mount Calvary Churches, in the field of Theological Education and Practical Wisdom in Ministry and Mission. For this, I congratulate him.

Hansel H. Henry, B. Phil., M. Min., D. Min.,

Executive Vice Bishop, Mount Calvary Holy Church of America Inc.

Chapter Five

The Ministry of an Evangelist

Biblically, evangelism is the clear proclamation of the gospel of Jesus Christ, leaving the results entirely up to the sovereignty of the Holy Spirit. Surely some have a special gift of evangelism, but their ministry does not excuse the responsibility of every Christian to communicate the gospel. Paul speaks to the church in Ephesians chapter three.

Unto me, who am less than the least of all saints, is this Grace given that I should preach among the Gentiles the unsearchable riches of Christ {Ephesians 3:8 AV}.

In the book of Acts, Luke wrote:

Therefore, they who were scattered abroad went everywhere preaching the Word {Acts 8:4 AV}.

Luke also mentioned that the church "went about preaching the word". Perhaps we can say that the church both has a mission in the world to take the gospel of Good News. The church's ministry is highly theological, producing discerning students of truth who are able—because of their understanding of truth—to detect and avoid error. It includes all people, the Jews or Gentiles, men and women, people of all colours on earth. Evangelism, therefore, is a major task of the church, a declared in the Great Commission (Matt. 28:18-20).

The word EVANGELIST means a messenger, who brings good tidings, that is, the "gospel". The word "evangelist" is from the Greek word "evangelistes" which denotes "a preacher of the gospel". The word originally—meant one who proclaims or brings good news or good tidings. The ministry of an evangelist is needed especially in our cities where many people have heard little or nothing of the Good News of Jesus Christ. An evangelist has an outgoing personality. He likes to meet people and share with them about Jesus. He has a burning desire to confront the lost with the gospel. He has a passion for souls—an evangelist is not limited to mass crusades, but he also witnesses on a one to one basis.

While every Christian should "evangelize" or be encouraged to do the work of an evangelist, the calling and gifting of an evangelist is not given to all. The distinctiveness of the calling, gifting and function of an evangelist is made clear in (Acts 21:8; Eph.4:11).

Evangelists are of great importance to the growth and well-being of the Body of Christ. A local Church that does not have or encourage the ministry of an evangelist will cease to grow physically. Every local Church should seek to have an evangelist who will help mobilise others into reaching the lost souls in the community.13. See also: Mark 16: 15-18; St. Luke 4: 18-19; Acts 21: 8; Eph. 4: 11; 2 Tim. 4: 5 etc.).

Preparing for the Ministry of an Evangelist

The obvious spiritual elements include such matters as faith, reliance upon prayer, the reality of the Holy Spirit in the life of an Evangelist, and the absolute authority of God's inerrant Word as the basis for leadership and ministry. However, to function in the office of an evangelist, one must have a definite call from God. His calling will be confirmed by other seasoned ministries and be recognised by the Body of Christ, especially in the circle of his influence. An evangelist needs to work from a local Church which will be to his advantage. The local Church will provide him with:

a. Prayer support

b. A body of accountability

c. Financial support, and etc.

d. A home base

One must be sure that:

a. He or she is a person of proven character and good works

b. He or she is committed to a local Church

c. He or she is full of the Holy Spirit and is of a sound mind

d. He or she is submissive to authority

e. He or she is grounded in the Word of God, having sound doctrine and not the spirit of deception

f. He or she must be one who can work with others without causing unnecessary divisions and schisms.

g. He or she welcomes other ministries to work with him or her

h. He or she must be one who adds souls to the local church, not one who scatters and brings confusion

i. He or she is one who knows his or her boundaries and limitations

j. He or she doesn't seek to do everything by himself or herself and for himself or herself

k. He or she is one that is willing to follow God's orders and directions

The Evangelist and his Ministry

When people have a genuine desire for the ministry, they are much more likely to think through the best ways to do it. This gives the individual the willingness to preach Christ, the hope of Glory, and not a humanistic propaganda (Acts 8: 5, 35). The vision of the evangelist is to seek and minister to the lost. His vision is broad but he or she should function closely with a local Church so that he or she can bring the lost into the Body of Christ to be nourished and established. He or she is, in a sense, a door into the Body of Christ or a bridge between the world and the local Church. An Evangelist should pass on the new converts to the caring Pastors and the Teachers of the Word. An Evangelist should train others to evangelise (Mark 16:15-20; Acts 8:5-8; 1Cor. 9:16; 2 Tim. 2:2). He must preach the true gospel that is not watered down by human ideologies. He should also preach salvation with love, cast out unclean spirits, heal the sick, set the captives free through the power of the Holy Spirit. He should be rich in the Word to avoid deception and misleading others. He should be sensitive to the voice of God in obedience and be willing to go where the Spirit leads (See Acts 8:26-40).

Examples of Evangelist Message

Men naturally may not be easily convinced without certain supernatural manifestations. When Philip went to Samaria, he preached Christ unto them. And in response, "The people with one accord gave heed unto those things which Philip spoke, hearing and seeking the miracles which he did. And there was great joy in that city" (Acts 8: 5-8). The people believed because "they saw and heard (of) the miracles which he did". This made them to acknowledge the fact that "Christ, indeed, is the Messiah".

In the Great Commission we are told:

And he said unto them, Go ye into all the world, and preach the gospel to every creature. He that believeth and is baptized shall be saved; but he that believeth not shall be damned. And these signs shall follow them that believe; In my name shall cast out devils; they shall speak with new tongues; They shall take up serpents; and if they drink any deadly thing, it shall not hurt them; they shall lay hands on the sick, and they shall recover. (Mark 16:15-18 AV; See also: Matt. 11:4-6; Luke 4:18; 9:1-2; 10:9, 17-19; Acts 3:1-10; 5:12-16; etc).

As certain of the gifts are specially designed for edification of the Church, so there are others that are ordained for the deliverance of men—both saints and sinners. Gifts such as word of wisdom, word of knowledge, gifts of healing, working of miracles and the gift of faith are specially useful in the ministry of deliverance. Without such charismatic gifts the work of deliverance may not be effective.

Reaching the Souls

Jesus was anointed to preach the gospel to the poor—He preached the message of hope and love. This is the period when God's mercies and favours are unlimitedly poured out for all who are willing to receive it. This message of hope is the backbone of all Evangelistic Ministry. Evangelists have a responsibility to reach the four corners of the world.

Prophet Isaiah foretold the Evangelistic Ministry of Jesus; he said:

The Spirit of the LORD God is upon me; because the LORD hath anointed me to preach good tidings unto the meek; he hath sent me to bind up the brokenhearted, to proclaim liberty to the captives, and the opening of the prison to them that are bound; To proclaim the acceptable year of the LORD, and the day of vengeance of our God; to comfort all that mourn; To appoint unto them that mourn in Zion, to give unto them beauty for ashes, the oil of joy for mourning, the garment of praise for the spirit of heaviness; that they might be called trees of righteousness, the planting of the LORD, that he might be glorified (Isaiah 61:1-3 AV).

Let us take note of these functions.

a. **To heal the broken-hearted**—Never before has there been such a great need in this area. We live in a world of wounded and broken hearts, people that are sick can only be touched miraculously by the power of the Word of God through His servants. And the LORD has promised to heal the wounds of His people (Jer.30:17).

Jesus restored the broken hearted, and today the work of an evangelist is to minister healing to these people, to minister to their emotional, spiritual and psychological needs (Acts 8v5-8).

b. **To preach deliverance to the captives**—Setting the captives free was the number one job that Jesus did everywhere He went in His ministry as an Evangelist. Some people are deceived into believing that demons do not exist today. You can not read and believe in the Bible and not believe in the existence of demonic powers in our modern world. The work of an Evangelist is to preach deliverance to those who are bound.

c. **Recovery of sight to the blind**—Jesus healed a lot of sick people including those that were both physically and spiritually blind. Physical healing and spiritual healing were both of equal importance to Him. In fact, every time He commissioned His disciples to go and preach the gospel, healing the sick was always included. Salvation is for the total man. Preaching alone will not do it. The yoke of bondage has to be broken by the anointing of the Holy Spirit and by the Word of God, which is able to pierce to joints and marrow.

d. **To set at liberty them that are bruised**—There are millions of people out there who are living hopeless—they have been bruised, bound and crushed by calamities. Through the evangelistic ministry, they can be set free and their lives set back into order.

Evangelistic Licensing that Mount Calvary Church will be using

The following risk management questions has been designed to help churches in effective. It is designed and adopted by our Church—Mount Calvary Church—and I believe it will be useful to other churches and ministries.

1. What is meant by the Pauline Epistles? How many are there?

2. What do you feel is the significance work of an Evangelist?

3. What are the gifts of the Spirit, and how do they operate in the church?

4. What is the significance of a Revival?

5. What is the significance of tithing?

6. What is faith?

7. What is meant by the Father, Son, and Holy Ghost?

8. What is the difference between the Holy Ghost and The Holy Spirit?

9. What is meant by the anointing?

10. What is meant by justification?

11. How many sons did Sceva have?

12. How do you prepare your sermons?

13. Should Holy Ghost ministers use notes when they preach?

14. What is meant by preaching for the occasion?

15. Should an Evangelist engage in Pastoral Counselling?

16. What are demons? Are they real? Can they be disposed of? Explain

17. What is meant by the term charismatic?

18. Name some areas of Evangelism besides the pulpit

19. Which of the local church leaders you understand to and what position do they hold?

20. Why do you want to move from holding a Minister's License to holding an Evangelistic License?

21. Discuss the advances in your Ministry since you received the Minister's Licence?

22. On an average, how much do you engage in Evangelism over a thirty day period (monthly?)

23. Interpret in your own words 2 Cornithian14: 32

24. Interpret in your own words Hebrew 13:1, 7.

25. Is to be called the same as being chosen? Explain

26. From a biblical point of view, explains the following:
    » Adultery
    » Fornication
    » Lasciviousness

27. Identify the following Biblical personalities:
    » Philip
    » Stephen
    » Darius
    » Agrippa
    » Festus
    » Apollos
    » Lydia
    » Barnabas
    » Rahab
    » Demetrius in OT
    » Saul in OT
    » Saul in NT

28. Identify the following Biblical places—what happened

- » Mount Ararat

- » Samaria

- » Mount Calvary

- » Mount Carmel

- » Babel

- » Antioch

29. Name the title of three spiritual books you have read recently, other than the Bible.

30. If called upon to speak /preach at the following week, name an appropriate text and subject for each:

- » Women's Day

- » Men's Day

- » Family Day

- » An appreciation service for senior leadership

- » Easter

- » Christmas

- » Thanksgiving

- » Annual Youth Day

- » Buildings Fund or Rally Day

31. Who wrote the Bible? Explain with Scriptures proof.

32. What is meant by the term homiletics

33. Discuss your options for expand or broaden your Evangelistic ministry. In order words share your vision, especially that part that has to do with your pursuit or quest for knowledge

Contributor

The author of this book: "Practical Policy Making and Job Description in Christian Ministry and Mission", Bishop Allan Miller, is a credible, God fearing servant of God. He teaches us, through this book, that we need to follow the ministry and leadership of Jesus in order to be able to lead as He desires for us to lead. We need to follow the example of the Apostolic Biblical Principles that Bishop Allan Miller writes about with so much spiritual and practical insight. The apostle Paul stated that principle well when he encouraged the Corinthians "Follow me as I follow Christ" {1 Corinthians 11:1}.

The book is a manual for ministry and it has appeared at such a time as this, when it seems the church does not know what it is doing, with regards to the fivefold ministry, the need to acknowledge the use of other gifts in running the church and the need for proper financial accountability. Without a doubt, our Lord is calling us to a distinctively Christ-centered kind of ministry and leadership. Quite to the contrary, we need committed Christian leaders and ministers who will lead by serving members of the ministry God has entrusted to them with passion and practical application how to do that.

The book acts as a guidebook for both Pastors and ministers in churches of all sizes and locations. The book reveals most of the practicalities of ministry. There are many things a minister learns along the road in caring for the flock of the Lord. This is a book for our time—and it is a book for leaders in every arena of Christian leadership, every minister will benefit from this comprehensive study of job description in Christian ministry in the 21st Century, incorporating the old apostolic order with our new technological order for a progressive church. I would recommend this book to every brother and sister in Christ Jesus in achieving the goals to the glory of God and to the advancement of His kingdom.

T. France, BA. MA, D. Th.,

Retired Teacher in Pastoral Theology

The Theological Seminary and Biblical Studies

Chapter Six

The Function of a Pastor

The word "Pastor" is a translation from the Greek word "poimen". It is the usual word for "Shepherd", but it is used for "pastor" only in (Eph.4:11). The English word "pastor" is from the Latin word "Pastorern" which means a shepherd. It only occurs in Eph. 4:11. Sixteen times it is translated as "Shepherd" in the New Testament (such as in John 10: 11; Heb. 13: 20; 1Peter 2:25, 5: 4). This designation clearly demonstrates the basic function of the pastoral ministry as "Shepherding"—the "flock" (poimmon) being a metaphor for the Church.

Take heed therefore unto yourselves, and to all the flock, over the which the Holy Ghost hath made you overseers, to feed the church of God, which he hath purchase with his own blood. For I know this, that after my departing shall grievous wolves enter in among you, not sparing the flock {Acts 20:28-29 AV}.

Feed the flock of God which is among you, taking the oversight thereof, not by constraint, but willingly; not for filthy lucre, but of a ready mind; neither as being lords over God's heritage, but being examples to the flock {1 Peter 5:2-3 AV}.

The pastor needs to work with others never succeeds beyond his limitations. A Pastor is one who oversees and cares for the spiritual needs of a local Church. He may also be called: 'Elder' (Acts 20: 17; Tit. 1: 5) or 'Overseer' (1Tim. 3: 1; Tit. 1: 7). He must lead with wisdom and must possess the ability to work with other, as he leads a team ministry.

A Pastor must have a shepherding spirit—he must be a leader who feeds, protects and oversees his flock. He guides the congregation and makes sure the congregation is spiritually nourished and protected and led in the right direction (1 Peter 5: 1-3). He works together with other ministries in establishing the local Church. A Pastor must learn to work not only with his elders and deacons, but also with evangelists, apostles, prophets and teachers to benefit his local congregation. (See Also: Eze.34: 3-5; Jer.3: 15; John 21: 16; Acts 20: 28 etc).

Biblical Guidelines for the Pastor

A Pastor as a leader of his local Church must meet the qualifications of an elder as established in God's Word (1Tim. 3; Tit.1). He must be a spiritual person with character and domestic qualifications. He needs to be a true shepherd, not just a hireling. He has to have a heart towards his people, open and honest. He needs to be able to share with the hurting members. His life must be open to the leading of the Chief Shepherd, the Lord Jesus, the giver of hope and life. (See also: Num. 27: 16-17; John 10: 1-27; 2Tim.4: 4; 1 Tim. 3: 1-6, etc).

The Pastor must be Prepared

Many Pastors fail in their ministry because they are poorly prepared for their ministry. The following are strongly urged:

1. Get into a good Bible School if possible. You can take a few classes as time allows. Or study with a correspondence school and listen to some good teachings of other successful Pastors.

2. Get a good reference Bible with other good study guides and spend time daily in God's Word.

3. Learn to express yourself intelligently—this will help increase the effectiveness of your ministry.

4. Give the Holy Spirit pre-eminence in your personal life. This will increase the spiritual authority and effectiveness in your ministry.

5. A Pastor must live in obedience to God. (See Jos. 1: 8; Matt. 16: 24; John 14: 23; Gal.2: 20 etc.)

6. The Pastor must be steadfast in his work. (See James 1: 6-8; 1 Peter 1: 13 etc.)

7. The Pastor must be honest in all matters. (See Prov. 10: 9; 1Cor. 4: 2; Gal. 5: 16; 1 John 1: 7 etc.)

8. The Pastor must be good a builder, not only building people's characters, homes and lives, but also building numbers in the Lord's House with the people the evangelist has given him. No Pastor should be content with the same number of people year after year.

Congregation should respond to its Pastor

a. The congregation should acknowledge their Pastor's position as their shepherd and accept his leadership.

b. Submit, honour and esteem him highly as a man or woman of God.

c. Pray for him and his family often

d. Individual members should find out whether he has any needs; then see whether they can help without advertising their good will to the public. This should be done as unto the Lord.

e. Always speaking well of your pastor to build his reputation. No members should ever be allowed to be use by the enemy to slander or tear down the man or woman of God. (Matt. 12:36).

f. Fellowship with him or her and encouragement of some kind will help.

g. Show him or her that he is loved and respected publicly.

Pastor Guidelines for the Team

The Pastor should give room to train and raise up his leadership to function in the Body. No Pastor should be too insecure to raise up others in ministry or to take time to work with others. Team ministry is when two or more people with ministry gifts join efforts to work together for the common good. God's pattern is for different ministries to work together in a team to bring the Body of Christ into perfection (1Peter 4: 10-11). A person who works alone never grows and overcomes weaknesses. He never learns to overcome the spirit of jealousy, insecurity and selfishness unless he learns to work with others. Some examples of team ministry include: Paul and Barnabas (Acts 13: 13-14); Paul and Silas (Acts 15: 40—16: 40); Peter and John

(Acts 8: 14-25); Prophets and Teachers in Antioch (Acts 13: 1-4); Bishops and Deacons (Phil. 1: 1).

Pastor's Local Organization or Church

1. The Church can only be organised by an authorised Local Pastor or the State Overseer or Bishop.

2. The Pastor is the only person authorised to call a business meeting in the local Church

3. All auxiliaries and boards such as Deacons and Trustees, etc., should make a full written report to the Pastor.

4. Pastor's should be checking and supervising the local Church in all ways.

5. Pastor shall preside at all business meetings, or his appointee.

6. The Pastor is authorised to perform all of the ordinances of the Church.

7. The Pastor should appoint necessary committees for the local Church and its work.

8. The Pastor has a charge from God to preach the Word and this he should do with power and spirit and without fear of favour.

9. As the Pastor or Shepherd of the flock, he should make pastoral visits and give special care to the sick, comfort the dying, etc.,

10. Pastor shall perform marriage ceremonies and counsel the newly-weds.

11. Exercising his Biblical authority, he is to reprove, rebuke and exhort with all long-suffering and doctrine.

12. Because he stands in Christ's stead, he is to seek the conversion of sinners, the sanctification of believers and the edification of the Church.[2]

13. It is the pastor's duty to train Christian works for ministry. This can be done in a number of ways:

---

2 See also: Harold I. Williams, The Mount Calvary Holy Church of America, Incorporated Manual, Washington: MCHCA, 1999, pp.2-8

- » Start by giving them small responsibilities with supervision. Their response and growth will determine how much more to give them.

- » Train them gradually, discipline them in the things of God.

- » Give them your confidence and trust, and encourage them.

- » Help them and give them another chance when they fall.

- » Communicate your vision to them in clear terms and keep them informed and up—to—date as your vision changes and grows.

Pastor & Elder Licensing that Mount Calvary Church will be using

The following risk management questions has been designed to help churches in effective. It is designed and adopted by our Church—Mount Calvary Church—and I believe it will be useful to other churches and ministries.

1. What is the significance of Eucharist
2. What is a liturgy
3. Interpret in your own words Acts 2: 47
4. Interpret in your own words Matthew 16:18
5. Interpret in your own words Ephesians 4: 5
6. What is a Call to Worship?
7. What is an Invocation
8. What is the significance of feet washing?
9. What is meant by the unleavened bread?
10. How essential is water baptism
11. Describe the various types of prayers

    - » Prayer of repentance
    - » Prayer of intercession
    - » Prayer of thanksgiving

12. What is meant by the Pentecostal experience?

13. What is the significance work of an Pastor

14. What is the significance work of an Assistant Pastor? Explain

15. What is meant by the fruit of the vine?

16. How many dispensations are there listed in the Schofield Bible? Name and describe three of them

17. Discuss the dedication of a child as set forth in the manual of your church organisation

18. Discuss the order of service for a funeral as set forth in the manual of your church organisation.

19. Discuss in detail, at least three of the offeneses for which a pastor may be liable to accusations as set forth in the Bible?

20. What is the purpose of Church discipline?

21. What is divine healing

22. What is the purpose of the church trustees board

23. Explain what is meant by the following terms:

   » Eulogy

   » Sermon

   » Sermonette

   » Lecture

   » Seminar

   » Workshop

   » Testimony

   » A fast

   » A shut-in

Contributor

I t has been a privilege and honour to be asked to provide a contributor to Dr Allan Miller, a man with a great heart for God and His people. The Bible, the book of all books, states in Hebrews 1:1-2 "God in sundry times and divers manner spoke in time past unto the father's by the Prophets has in these last days spoken unto us by His Son Jesus Christ". God's Son has spoken to the spirit of the Most Honourable, Right Reverend Dr Allan P Miller, to pen principles upholding the sacred calling of ministry deep in his heart, and embracing in servanthood, a desire to empower God's people.

The author of this book: "Practical Policy Making and Job Description in Christian Ministry and Mission" have been known to me as Bishop, lecturer, friend and brother in Christ for the past eight years as a credible, God fearing servant of God whose passion is to see the work of the ministry advancing, by first applying the Biblical Principles and secondly by applying some of our 21st Century technological principles to run an effective church.

Dr Miller is no stranger to a lecture hall, no outsider to preaching to masses, and is no foreigner to mentoring ministers internationally. Yet, sovereign timing has Dr Miller sharing with all walks of life, to deepen their convictions of faith through print.

I am impressed with Dr Miller's acquired level of knowledge in the Word of God, and also in the secular world, and yet still maintains a great spirit of humility towards God and fellowmen.

This treasure chest of literature will be an asset in your home library and a beacon throughout your discipleship with the Lord. I pray that through this book, God will help you and your Church in the 21st Century, incorporating the old apostolic order with our new technological order for a progressive church. I would recommend this book to every minister who wants to do ministry well to the glory of the Lord.

John A Walker, M. Th., D. Th.,

International Executive Councilman of Triumphant Church of God

Brampton, Ontario: Canada

Chapter Seven

The Ministry of a Teacher

The major task of a teacher is to teach the Word of God entrusted to him and faithfully point the Body of Christ to sound and life-giving doctrine. The teaching ministry seems to be the most flexible of all the ministry gifts. It is possible to be a Pastor—Teacher, Evangelist—Teacher, Prophet—Teacher or Apostle—Teacher. For example, Paul was an Apostle—Prophet—Teacher—Evangelist and etc. One does not become a Teacher because of his natural abilities, but because of the divine calling upon his life. A Teacher should not rely on excellency of speech and the human intellect alone but on the inspiration of the Holy Spirit.

It is the power of the Holy Spirit, not mere head knowledge that brings life. (1Thess.1:5; 1Tim. 1:11-14; 1 John 2: 20-27) A teacher has a revelation gift that brings new thoughts and insights on the Scriptures. He accumulates and gives out the information to people, that makes God's Word come alive with power to the point of changing people's lives.

A Teacher should always hold fast to the Word of God, giving exposition on the Scriptures instead of on human philosophies which may seem right or appealing. He should seek every opportunity possible to impart the Word of God to others. Teacher should himself be well instructed, well equipped in rightly dividing the Word of God. It is a shame to see a Teacher that is poorly equipped trying to teach others. Example, would you allow a mechanic to work in your mouth? Or would you use a plumber to design your house?

"Teacher" came from the word "Didaskalos" from the word "Didasko", 'to teach'. It is frequently rendered "Master" in the four Gospels, as a title of address to Christ, while the word "Rabbi" or "Rabbei", from a word rab, which signifies signified "My Master" and was a title of respect by which teachers were addressed in the New Testament. Also the word "Rabbounei" or "Rabboni" formed in a similar way to the above, it was even more respectful than Rabbi, and signified "My Great Master". It is used in the New Testament addressed to Christ by blind Bartimaeus, and in St. John 20: 16 by Mary Magdalene.

Difference between Preaching and Teaching

- Preaching

Ten different preachers may preach from the same Scriptural text and use the same principles of preaching, and yet, preach ten sermons that are distinctly different. Such is the nature of art or skills. Preaching is not an act, a show, or a circus, but neither should it be boring or dull. It must have good taste to prevail, it must be creative, presented in interesting, informative and inspiring way. Preaching must go beyond informing and instructing. It must challenge the hearers to decide for or against the message. And, more importantly, the preacher must be "anointed" to preach.

- Teaching

Teaching seeks to impart information, give instructions and to inspire change. It seeks to affect change in an individual's thoughts, attitude and behaviour. The listening aspect of teaching will help you understand how people think, the kinds of real life experiences they encounter and the kinds of questions, doubts and fears they feel. Teaching will help you develop greater knowledge of and appreciation for the background—teaching gives practice in speaking before groups, help you "think on your feet", and gives practice in connecting the facts and principles of the Bible with the problems and tragedies of everyday life. "Practice, practice, practice"! That's how we develop from amateur to professional preaching or teaching status—practice, practice, practices. In the Mount Calvary Church Family context this means, 'Whatever you profess to being able to do, you should always be ready to do it'.

A good Teacher

A Teacher is one who has a special spiritual gift that enables him to clarify, expound and proclaim God's truth in order to cause understanding and to build the Body of Christ. The ministry of teaching is very essential to the building and the perfecting of the saints. Teachers are devoted to giving God's people instruction and understanding of the written Word. They teach to restore God's truth. They teach to unite the Body of Christ. Teachers help bring believers to full maturity. A local Church or believer that rejects the teachings of godly men and women of God will stop growing and will soon become a victim of misconception and lack of truth. Believers that receive sound teachings and put them into practice are saved from false human ideologies. Sound teachings produce in them spiritual authority and make their walk with the Lord more worthwhile.

It is crucial for believers to be well instructed and established in the objective truth of the written Word. The Word is our only offensive weapon against the enemy. This makes the Teachers generally tend to be more technical, systematic and precise. This could seem boring to some people who are used to fiery preaching. It is very important to understand that teaching must play a prominent role in the church if we are to be well instructed. It should be noted that Teachers were well received in the time of Jesus. Among the Jewish people, they were called "masters" or "lords". Among all the titles that Jesus had, He was best known during His time on earth as a great teacher. Jesus loved to teach because it is through this noble ministry that the truth of God is restored or imparted to the people of God. See also: Matt. 4: 23; 9: 35; St. John 3: 2; Rom.12: 4—7; 1Corn.12: 28; Eph. 4: 11; James 3: 1).

Making or Examining the Teacher

One of the responsibilities of a Teacher is to safeguard the truth of God's Word from corruption and to make disciples that will keep the truth going. A Teacher should not act as if he knows everything. He should keep an open mind. When we talk about a teaching ministry, we are not talking about a Sunday School Teacher or a minister of Religious Education. The teacher is not appointed or elected by men for a period of time. Rather, the Teacher functions in a divine gift from God, is confirmed and recognised by the leadership and the Body of Christ. He should not lose sight of other people's needs. He should not be critical of those who differ from him in doctrine. But should make his teachings practical and simple to understand! See also: Jos. 1: 8; Ps. 1: 1-3, 119: 97; 1John 4: 1; 2 Peter 2: 1-3; Rev. 2: 20).

Pitfalls that every Teacher should avoid

Books and teachings are not the goals—they are only the means to achieve the goals. This can sometimes make one detached from the reality of life. Teachers should seek to be practical in their teachings. Teachings that impart life, like Paul's teachings to the Churches, always concludes with practical applications. Teachers must watch out not to rely on human wisdom. Teachers must be careful to allow the Holy Spirit to illuminate their understanding. The fresh anointing upon their teaching is of great importance.

It is sad when a teacher only teaches old messages and no longer receives anything fresh from the Lord. He depends on the old anointing instead of seeking for a new fresh anointing from the Lord. We are lacking a proper balance between move in the spiritual gifts and the solid, practical ground provided by the Word of God. (Prov. 3: 7. St John 7: 16-17; 1Corn. 2: 5-7).

The Authority of the Teacher

Teaching was and is a prominent part of the Early Church ministry. Teachers arrest attention, fasten home the truth by plain but profound instruction. The forceful authority of the teacher bears reference to the hearers, example Jesus. His authority was demonstrated as follows:

1. The astonishment of the teaching in St. Matt 7: 28-29.
2. The effect of the teaching in St. Mark 6: 2.
3. The people adored Jesus for His teaching St. Luke 4: 15.
4. The people were more of amazement at Jesus teaching St. John 7: 15.

The people 'wondered at the gracious words which proceeded out of his mouth' Luke 4: 22.

His authority as a Teacher was welcome by common people. Peter said "Lord, to whom shall we go? You have the words of eternal life . . ." The life must reflect the doctrine proclaimed—Teaching cannot be separated from ministry life.

Contributor

The author of this book: "Practical Policy Making and Job Description in Christian Ministry and Mission" has been known to me as Bishop Allan Miller from 2007 as a credible gift from God. As we approach the 21st Century, one problem continues and perhaps even magnifies itself in the churches and leadership vacuum all around us. That problem centers in a misunderstanding of ministerial roles that causes people and organizations to focus on individuals, prophets who will lead them out of the wilderness and into the Promised Land. And, sadly, most people have been led astray by false teachers or prophets.

The problem is they haven't been trained. And this book gives us some key factors to help us serve better and be more effective in our ministerial roles. The book has been written with simplicity, so that everyone involved in ministry can understand and benefit from it. Yet, it is profound and practical, loaded with depths of Scriptural and theological truths. Moreover, Dr. A. Miller is a Pentecostal Scholar, minister and theologian, his book is beneficial for every Evangelical minister—irrespective of his or denomination. Furthermore, he has expanded this book well beyond the boundaries of the local church.

I have made great efforts to read the book thoroughly, and I strongly recommend it to all Christians who are in ministry and leadership. It is also a valuable text book for students and teachers in Bible School or Seminary.

G. Murray, BA. M Min, D.D.

Teacher of Christian Literature, at the Leadership Seminary

Chapter Eight

The Ministry Role of a Church Secretary

Minutes are vital to the success of every meeting whether in the secular or in the church organisation. Participants rely on them for information on subjects they did not understand or to fill in gaps when they lost concentration. The action points act as a reminder to those who agreed in the heat of the moment but have since been overtaken by other priorities and would otherwise forget what they were to do. Those who could not attend need an idea of what was decided in their absence. And finally, minutes are the historical record of the meeting and 'proof' of the actions / outcomes.

This is what the Minor Prophet Habakkuk said, in chapter two:

And the LORD answered me, and said, write the vision, and make it plain upon tables, that he may run that readeth it. For the vision is yet for an appointed time, but at the end it shall speak, and not lie: though it tarry, wait for it; because it will surely come, it will not tarry {Habakkuk 2:2-3AV}.

In ancient times records were kept for future references or for remembrance. After the defeat of the Amalekites by Israel, the LORD commanded Moses: "Write this for a memorial in a book" {Exod.17:14 AV}. Prophet Jeremiah was instructed by God to "Write thee all the Words that I have spoken unto thee in a book" {Jer.30:2 AV}. It is the view of most scholars that Baruch, who wrote some of Jeremiah's prophecies, was the prophet's personal secretary or scribe.

Then Jeremiah called Baruch the son of Neriah: and Baruch wrote from the mouth of Jeremiah all the words of the LORD, which he had spoken unto him, upon a roll of a book {Jeremiah 36:4 AV}.

Again: And they asked Baruch, saying, tell us now, how didst thou write all these words at his mouth? Then Baruch answered them, He pronounced all these words unto me with his mouth, and I wrote them with ink in the book {Jeremiah 36: 17-18 AV}.

In her Song of Thanksgiving, after Sisera was killed, Deborah paid tributes to everyone involved in the battle. She pond special tributes to the tribe of Zebulun, which produced the "writers", who kept records of the ongoing war. She said, "Out of Zebulun they that handled the pen of the writer" {Jud. 5:14 AV}. Those who "handled the pen of the writer" were skilled in recording events with clarity and accuracy. A church's secretary may not be a preacher or good as a speaker, but he or she is skilled in handling "the pen of the writer".

For a role that carries significant responsibility, there is very little support for the minute-taker. There is a common misconception that secretaries can take minutes. In fact, a secretary is only a little more likely to be trained to take minutes than to be a company secretary. Ask secretaries what they are typing and they are likely to have to look at it before answering—typing does not involve the brain on a conscious level; shorthand is similarly a mechanical skill, and so is scribbling the words that someone says.

The key skill for taking minutes is the ability to listen to the words someone is saying, absorb them, evaluate the manner of the delivery and identify the speaker's points of views—the message. It is ongoing listening and simultaneous summarising of the knowledge of given information.

There is a second type of minute—take people who attend to contribute but find themselves taking the notes in the absences of a secretary. Few have received any training, and although many have been taking minutes for years, the lack of clear focus and structure for the meeting has made them wonder about the 'theory' behind the practice. Meetings that are well run are appreciated by everyone, and the minute-taker plays a large part in achieving this. Although it is the chairperson who 'fronts' and controls the meeting, it is the support of the minute-taker that enables this to be done effectively. Just has God controlled His meeting and telling Moses what must into the minute-take.

And the LORD said unto Moses, write thou these words: for after the tenor of these words I have made a covenant with thee and with Israel. And he was there with the Lord forty days and forty nights; he did neither eat bread, nor drink water. And he wrote upon the tables the words of the covenant, the Ten Commandments {Exodus 34:27-28AV}.

In most organisations, there are no 'rules' for minutes: some want formality, others a more casual style; some all the detail, others only a list of action points. Any guidance is usually limited to house style for layout, not content. The minute-taker has to be flexible, sensitive and responsive to the needs of both the chairperson and the group.

The minute-taker is one of the most important and powerful people in the meeting. Although the task can be daunting, it is the opportunity to develop your knowledge, broaden your horizons and build your credibility within the organization. With a clear idea of your role and responsibilities, knowledge of what you are meant to do and some confidence in yourself, your role of minute-taker can even be enjoyable!

A meeting can be a positive or negative experience, depending on the skill of the chairperson and the attitude of those attending. A meeting that is badly structured and uncontrolled will definitely be stressful and frustrating and will waste far more time than just the allotted span. There is far more to the meeting than just the time spent around the table.

1. In order to be successful, everyone must:
2. Know why they are there
3. Recognise what is to be achieved
4. Have read all the paperwork in advance
5. Be prepared mentally and practically
6. Willing to contribute positively
7. Willing to listen to and learn from others
8. Focus and keep to the point
9. Leave with a clear understanding of any points they should put into action.

Arranging a meeting:

In theory setting up a meeting should present no problem: a few phone calls, a confirmation note's or email and that's it. Anyone who has tried to do it knows the reality: endless calls trying to find mutually convenient dates, difficulty in booking rooms, and the cost that go with it. Once the date and place have been agreed on, the next step is so important, to cycle the agenda.

1. Draft of the agenda

2. Approved of the agenda dispatched

3. Deadline for the agenda.

Before you begin to arrange the meeting find out who the 'priority people' are—those without whom the meeting cannot go ahead. Select a few dates, spreading them across different days and weeks and times of the day and then email them or fax everyone with a 'notice of agenda' explaining why the meeting is being held and offering dates.

1. Why they are attending

2. What will be asked of them?

3. Where their involvement fits into the overall objective of the meeting.

4. Who else will be present?

5. Plan for the future.

It is important to state here that every church meeting—whether formal or informal should begin and end with a word of prayer. The prayer should not be a "sermon" or a summary of all the points discussed, but concise and, of course, spiritual.

Recording decisions and actions

A significant part of the reason for having minutes is to record the decisions,

A significant portion of the reason for having minutes is to provide record for the relevant decision that are taken and to remind the participants of what they agreed to do. If the minutes from the previous meeting are available to fulfil this purpose, they need to be able to sent out promptly and with actions clearly marked. It is essential that you leave the meeting knowing exactly what the best outcomes, the action points, are—the action triangle.

1. Precisely what is going to be done?
2. Who will help take responsibility?
3. When the action should be considered completed.

Most people do not read minutes in any great depth. They are more concerned about the people present and the headline of what is being said at the meeting. But they are not much interested in the detail and the actions required of them. These readers are likely to miss actions that are buried within a paragraph, so the action must be a separate paragraph, even if it is just a few words.

1. Layout

The layout of your minutes is very vital. People are generally not that much interested in them anyway, so make them look readable and interesting to tempt them to at least skim through. There is also the option aspect that people judge the content by the appearance, so if they look a mess, the reader won't trust the content.

2. Page layout

Indention is the most commonly preferred style because it is easier to read and the layout reinforces the relative importance of the information.

3. Avoid personal attack

a. Again listen for the points being made rather than the style.
b. Be careful about contentious words.
c. Maintain a neutral attitude, avoid partiality

4. Don't show the mood

Avoid phrases like 'after heated debates '.

5. Don't judge

Your opinion should not come through in the tone of the minutes with phrases like 'the committee eventually decided to ...' or after lengthy brief discussion.

6. Confidential information

Remember a confidential item is confidential.

7. Action points

a. Ensure that the action is shown as being the responsibility of a defined member of the group.

b. State precisely what that person is to do.

c. Give a clear deadline for the action.

One of the toughest jobs in a church is that of the church secretary. A church secretary can be an asset to a pastor / leadership; he or she can also ruin a church ministry. There are some attributes for a secretary other than office skills that many forget to consider. These are a few qualities to consider in a church secretary.

1. **Discreet:** Another way to say this is "selective amnesia", he or she needs to be able to forget certain information easily. A prospective church secretary is privy to the confidential information intended from counselling sessions to tithe records. It is essential that the one in this category be able to forget what he or she knows when seeing the individual in worship service. Please note there should be no change in your behaviour towards an individual because of what you known.

2. **Trustworthy:** The church secretary needs to be able to keep "secrets". Confidential information does not belong on the church's

prayer tree as gossip. Many things that are said in the church office or members meeting do not need to be repeated to others at any time. The secretary has been entrusted with these matters and he or she should demonstrate trustworthiness.

3. **Protector:** A great church secretary will protect the pastor's and the leadership team's reputation. He or she should make sure that there is no question regarding the status or relationship between pastor or leadership team and the secretary. During counselling sessions with a woman, if the pastor or leadership team's wife is not available, the church secretary should remain at least in the outer office if not asked to be in the session itself. No opportunity to malign the reputation of the both persons should be allowed.

4. **Know his or her limits:** Not everyone who is a church secretary can handle all the latest business of the church; however, he or she should be willing to learn if asked. Depending on the size of the church, certain amount of business aspects may need to be separated. A prospective church secretary also needs to be aware of what the pastor or leadership team wants he or her to handle and what needs his attention. A prospective church secretary should never assume responsibilities that are not disclosed or distributed even directly given to him or her by the pastor or leadership.

These indicate some of the common misconceptions concerning the role of the church secretary. The emphasis is on the church's secretary and this gives an insight or idea of the immense scope of the job. No two church secretaries will see their responsibilities in the same way. It is essentially clear therefore that the responsibilities of the church secretary will be unique to your own church. Hopefully, however, this study will help you find or think through some of the aspects of being a good church secretary.

Could this possibly be your calling?

The work of a secretary should be viewed as a "minister", and the secretary as a "minister". In addition to the qualities already discussed, a church secretary should be:

1. **Proficient:** Gifts of leadership, encouragement and inspiration are needed, together with an ability to see issues through. Much

appreciated time and energy efficiency are needed as change is managed, vision is sought and mission implemented. The church secretary will have a key role in this, together with other members of leadership.

2. **Pastoral:** It is essential that the church secretary should have a pastoral heart. The list of relationship between the church secretary and the minister is very vital and that needs to be nurtured. There will also be privileged need for confidentiality and trust in areas of church development, conflict and individual pastoral needs.

3. **Positive:** A church secretary with a positive attitude is a great asset to the pastor and the church as a whole. This positive disposition on will positively contribute to the life and future mission of the church and create a positive environment for excellence in the church. The church will find that such an amazing attitude will rub off on the other leaders and the strength of the congregation as a whole. The church secretary, like all leaders, will need to develop a healthy amnesia for past problems, failures and conflicts. It is essential that you remember that the church has a decision making process. The church secretary's role is to facilitate and work with the church councils and not to approve or reject such decisions. The church secretary will often be the first point of contact or correspondence. Along with the minister the church secretary is often seen as the first or key contact person.

Mount Calvary Church Appointment of Secretary

The church constitution should be set up with the procedure. As those listed to fill these roles need to have the confidence of their fellow office bearers, it probably is best that a nomination should be made by the office bearers in the church.

The best person available should be appointed to the task. The best way of organizing or achieving this is to educate the church about the roles of a church secretary, as to what qualities and skills are required for such role so that they will make sure their choice knowledgeably. One way of organizing or providing this information knowledge is to draw up a job description of the church secretary's office before any nominations are sought, and letting it be known what this is.

There are ways in which they can get involved to do their work better, though they will not pretend to possess the professional skills they do not possess. They can be encouraged to take on courses or study from books if they are lacking in professional skills or knowledge such as typing, or book—keeping. Church secretary work demands more than just professional privilege skills, there is much more to the task than technical support knowledge. The work of a church secretary includes:

1. Acting as Consultant

A church secretary needs to be a separate source of information. Many people will turn to him or her with questions about the respective church work, the church, its organizations, the international board administrator and the other local church authorities.

2. Publicizing

While much of his or her work or message should be delegated, the church secretary will often see that what is happening, or about to happen, is fully furnished by the people who need to know.

3. Delegating

If the answer to the whole church is to be the body of Christ, and all members are invited to be utilized in the ministry, the action secretary, from his or her position and with his or her knowledge has a strategic part to play.

Contributor

Being aware of the importance of this book to each of our brothers and sisters in Christ, I have observed the safe and coherent way of format, but behind these words is a living example that brings ministerial Bishop Allan P Miller, take to Birmingham: England community and each mission which I has visited. And it is there where I testify that hard ministerial work done together with his family and his community of Mount Calvary Church.

Since Bishop Allan and I met some years ago in London: England, at the consecration of the Right Rev Dr Mohan Lal, Bishop of Bethesda Apostolic Church in India. I saw Bishop Allan who was teaches patiently but primarily their responsibility it leads with joy. In this book we can learn to organize and discipline in multiple aspects that lead people to develop a ministerial to be efficient in the communication of God's Word to a people seeking leaders accountable and this is the point master of this book, it gives us a key to adjust the doors of all Apostolic Christian Church.

Responsibility is a virtue in love for the mission been encomendad us. It is a call to teach salvation from multiple of view the good news, lyrics and vocals done by every son and daughter of God. It is here that reading this book is synthesized functions from biblical perspective and not allow us to fall into a burucratica of faith.

In the world of marketing administration responsibilities in the manufacture of a product it is rigorous and essential to cover the Espectrum which aims, but at the ministerial exercise should be very clear that function must first fulfill basic principles that must exert to begin this process of sanctification to the people we are called to multiply the talents entrusted to us. In this book you can glimpse the way of clear, simple and above all with historical basis that is efficient biblical Word of Our Savior Jesus Christ.

Juan Gomez, BA, B. Phil., LLB,

Bishop of Anglican Church of Latin America

Chapter Nine

The Ministry of the Church Treasurer

The Role of the Church Treasurer

The ministry of the church's Treasurer is one of managing, safeguarding, and maintaining the financial resources entrusted to the church by the congregation and others to carry out its mission and vision. The role of the church treasurer can appear to be daunting, not helped by the lack of clear guidance as to what exactly is required which will vary considerably between size of the ministry or organization. In the majority of cases the role is carried out by a volunteer, although some ministries or organizations are beginning to consider employing someone with professional skills to carry out the duties. The treasurer is an officer of the church, an official position, serving the church by providing financial leadership at a strategic level.

The success of the church's treasurer comes from being a good manager of God's financial resources and provisions. When the treasurer appropriately managers the Church's—and God's—resources, God abundantly blesses the Church and rewards the faithful treasurer. This is what Jesus meant, when He said:

His lord said unto him, well done, thou good and faithful servant: you have been faithful over a few things, I will make you ruler over many things: enter thou into the joy of your Lord {Matthew 25:21 AV}.

A minister holds a position of leadership as a servant and representative of God to the flock {the people}. This position carries with it the vital challenge of an exemplary stewardship of time, talents and treasure. Pentecostal church leaders are beginning to appreciate the importance of financial integrity and accountability, which were often neglected in the past. Our giving wasn't the real problem; not having a budget was. We had no idea where our money was going, making our church ministry to be characterised by a consumer mentality. Priorities were often based on wants and desires instead of needs. Moreover, our leaders spent Church money {God's money} unwisely and selfishly, as though the money were theirs. Thankfully, this attitude is gradually changing, though much work needs to be done. Unfortunately, many Christian church leaders, including those in ministry, place their confidence in money and material things. This mind-set has already changed the hearts and lifestyles of too many Christians. God's people are entrusted with the privilege of setting an example of being the best possible managers of life and possessions.

It is an honour and privilege to manage Church's money. Every minister entrusted with God's money must prove themselves faithful and trustworthy. Those called into sacred ministry must not be money minded or motivated by monitory gains. In these days of over-emphasis on material prosperity, some erroneously believe that wealth determines personal. Godliness, "supposing that gain is godliness" (1 Tim.6:5). And as Paul has warried, "the love of money is source of all evils" (1 Tim. 6:20).

While the Church must not condemn wealth—because it is a blessing from God (Deut.8:18) to be received with thankfulness—it must not be allowed to distract or compromise our devotion and faithfulness to Jesus Christ. The proper attitude of the minister towards money is contentment. This will demonstrate that their primary motivating factor is not monitory gains, but their love for the Master. The minister should find contentment in Christ Jesus, as the source of his supply, and accept God's provision with gratitude and humility of heart.

For we brought nothing into this world, and it is certain we can carry nothing out. And having food and raiment let us be therewith content {1 Timothy 6:7-8 AV}.

The role of a church treasurer involves ensuring that there are essential controls and procedures in place for the proper management of charitable funds. This includes keeping detailed and accurate accounting records and reports of stewardship income, offerings, special appeals and any trading and restricted income; as well as detailed, receipted and categorised support records of expenditures. The treasurer is an officer or minister of the church, serving the church by providing financial leadership at a strategic level. He or she is appointed by the church with the support of the minister and officer board of the church.

The treasurer must act as the first and primary tier of financial checks and balances; and is responsible for the proper disbursement of church funds—both restricted and unrestricted within policies established by the Charity Commission, the church organization, also local church ministry. Serving in this role requires patience, accuracy and the fear of God.

God's treasurer must be faithful with God's money. Nehemiah appointed faithful men, men of integrity and financial accountability, as treasurers. God blessed his ministry and his treasurers. Nehemiah said: "And I made treasurers over the treasuries . . . for they were counted faithful" (Nehemiah 13:13 AV).

We are also told of unfaithful treasurers, who were dishonest and covetous; Judas Iscarriot was one of such men. He was the treasurer during Christ's ministry on earth {John 13:29}. But, unfortunately, Judas was "a thief"; he often dipped into the disciple's money for his own use {John 12:6}. There are many treasurers in our churches today, who reflect wrong attitude like that of Judas. Church money should be clearly separated from personal money. Both should never be mixed, under any circumstances.

The treasurer, as does the secretary, needs to be trustworthy more than his or her own name suggests. To him or her, the church should be able to turn for guidance in regard to the task of forecasting potential contributions of the membership, managing church resources and the most effective ways of using the resources for church projects. But more than this he or she needs to view money through spiritual eyes, from the point of view Christian stewardship, and see how it can be transmuted into lives won for Christ's Kingdom and the church. This will mean that he or she will not think of his or her role as that of simply guarding the church purse to stop people from irresponsible spending—though he or she will guard against incautious and unwise expenditure—but rather of being used to facilitate Christ's work.

He or she will therefore:

a. Use his or her knowledgeable abilities to present to the members the case for responsible Christian giving.

b. Know or get to know, where best to invest money, and make it earn as much as possible.

c. Be sure aware of the best way of organising borrowing money if the need arises.

d. Encourage people's support for the Lord's work on a worldwide basis and in particular the work of the church ministry.

It is the treasurer's duty to determine appropriate priorities. He or she should be prudent enough not to allow a church ministry which appears urgent to take priority over the important. The treasurer and team should establish mutually acceptable budgeting and spending priorities. As a treasurer, it will help to make sure that you keep your ministry and heart free from the temptations relating to money and be content with what you have, because God has said:

Let your conversation be without covetousness and be content with such things as you have for He has said, I will never leave you, nor forsake you {Hebrew 13:5 AV}.

A contented treasurer strives to have godly priorities, live a reasonable life-style and be a thankful giver. A hoarding attitude often comes from dwelling on the 'what ifs?' of the ministry future. But Paul said:

For God has not given us the spirit of fear but of power and of love and of a sound mind {2 Timothy 1:7 AV}.

I recommend the following guidelines for managing Church's finance, which have been effectively adopted by Mount Calvary Church:

a. The timing of salary payments and method of payment.

b. In what way the church minister presents the note of his or her expenses, and at what point in the month.

c. It must be agreed beforehand if NI, Tax, or pension contributions, etc., are to be deducted.

d. Ensure that the method by which the church will review the level of detail salary is acceptable and duly implemented. In this regard the church treasurers should be aware of what the church board or officers have recommended.

e. Any increase in stipends should also be taken into consideration.

Many church congregations provide adequate compensation for their ministers, but others do not. A church financial remuneration for its leader doesn't necessarily reflect its love for him or her. Small church congregations often struggle to provide ministers with adequate incomes. That's why I'm so convinced that everyone, regardless of income level, should live on a budget. A budget's purpose is to free a person, not confine. Proverbs record:

A man's heart devises his way: but the Lord directs his steps {Proverbs 16:9 AV}.

There are very practical reasons for having a budget. A budget can free the planner from worrying about

1. Making the annual insurance payment

2. Having money put aside for taxes or the mortgage, etc

3. Having money available for supplies and difficult times

This treasurer budget is a plan that can help both individual Christian and the whole church to manage their money and live within their means. When a budget is developed with the goal of becoming free from the bondage of debt, a person quickly learns the benefits of following God's truth and receiving His promises.

Though the Board of Directors and others in the church—counters, budget teams, stewardship committees, etc. —all share responsibility as stewards of church assets and financial operations, it is the Treasurer who has the specific responsibility of day-to-day management of the church's financial resources. These include:

1. Faithful financial management with a budget maximizes the benefits of any surplus. Wise use of provisions serves the best interests of a treasurer's role and establishes a good stewardship pattern for his or her church congregation.

2. Keep a list of ongoing list monthly fixed expenditures. These include salary taxes; household expenses; mortgage or rent; insurance; and so on.

3. List of variable expenses. This includes food, utilities, transportation, debt repayments, insurance, clothing, medical, training and others.

4. List all available income. This includes tithe, interest and dividends, income tax refunds, and any other income sources.

5. Those on a non-fixed income. If it's necessary to work part-time to supplement income.

I have found this Scriptural guidelines for budgeting to be useful, in the book of {Proverbs 27:23}. The writer has admonished:

Be you diligent to know the state of your flocks, and look well to your herds {Proverbs 27:23 AV}.

Budgets are very simple: a specific amount of money is designated for spending, and a budget gives direction for spending it. Nevertheless, even in a small church ministry this role is so important with their expertise and advice. So the Candidates for Treasurer should be members of the Board of Directors, as elected by the congregation. Usually, the position of Treasurer is elected by and within the Board itself. The Treasurer is accountable to the congregation through its relationship to the Board of Directors and acts on authority granted the position by church by-laws and the Board.

Core Competencies of a Treasurer

One does not have to be an accountant or bookkeeper to be a good church treasurer. However, there are several qualities necessary to be successful in the position.

1. Honesty and trustworthiness—the congregation must have complete confidence in the one who manages their gifts to God's church.

2. Well-organized—the Treasurer is responsible for ensuring that many tasks are completed, both accurately and in a timely manner; organization and attention to detail is critical.

3. Willingness to learn and seek guidance—those coming to the Treasurer's position without formal accounting or bookkeeping training must become familiar with basic accounting principles, as well as the financial operating procedures specific to their local church. If the policies and procedures are non-existent or

incomplete, it is the responsibility of the Treasurer to request that the church address such issues as soon as possible.

4. Commitment—the Treasurer's job is time-consuming. Even though a number of tasks can and should be delegated to others, it remains the Treasurer's responsibility to ensure that those tasks are completed in an accurate and timely fashion. This may require up to six or more hours per week.

5. Ability to work well with others—A significant part of the Treasurer's responsibilities involves interacting with others within the church, for example, the other members of the Board, church staff, various committee members, volunteers, and individuals in the congregation. The Treasurer should be able to confidently convey information, delegate necessary tasks, and direct and empower volunteers in a courteous, agreeable manner.

In order to avoid conflicts of interest and maintain proper controls the various duties of treasurer, cashier and stewardship recorder should be separated where possible. In a larger church a separate accountant may be appointed under the management of the treasurer. Larger churches are also required to maintain a risk register; various activities may carry a financial risk.

He or she therefore, needs to be trustworthy and efficient. It should be noted that simple lack of care knowledge in handling money has probably been a greater cause of scandal in the church than downright dishonesty. This means that, not because anyone distrusts him or her, there must be enabled accepted procedures for checking.

I think this would be helpful.

1. Record all transactions immediately. It is essential clear practice to carry a notebook for this purpose.

2. Give receipts. These include or should be issued for all money received (apart from Sunday and other offerings) to ensure that the information counterfoils are kept up for audit. Once again make sure that collections at services are properly recorded. It is essentially important and wise always to have a witness to count and been countersign the entry of the amount in an "offering record book".

3. Get a receipt for all your payments. This is a wise thing to do even though the payment is made by credit card or bank transfer or cheques. They should be kept in order of preference payment. Where cash is given to the ministers of any kind for or of benevolent purposes they should sign a receipt for it and be asked to provide or keep a private record of disbursements. It is best for all payments to be made against invoices or {in the case of expenses} receipts. If possible always make payments by cheque rather than cash.

4. Have a clear but simple bookkeeping system:

   a. Cash book which records all payments and receipts. Expenses should be paid for actual expenses incurred and not be a set amount each month either to the minister or to anyone else. Lump sum payment may incur tax liabilities.

   b. Cash analysis ledger as the basis for preparing statement of accounts.

   c. Record of all bank lodgement.

5. Pay all accounts quickly. However, a church should pay its accounts immediately. The testimony of the church is at stake. Establish and maintain complete and up-to-date wage, tax, National Insurance and, if appropriate, pension contributions records. Also submit quarterly PAYE and NI tax filling on time.

6. Ensure that you balance your books regularly. The longer this task is left the more difficult it becomes. It is essential clear to work monthly. Bank statement should be obtained at least quarterly basis and a reconciliation made. Then prepare and present at least quarterly financial reports to the church board. These should include income and expenditure, cash-flows and balance sheet / statement of assets and liabilities. Ideally these should be shown against the budget and for the same period last year.

7. Never mix personal and church funds. This rule must be adhered to in connection with both cash and bank accounts. There is also the option risk that if the treasurer should die no one would expect or know what was what and the church bank account could be frozen.

8. Submit all records to an auditor. The church should appointed auditors each year to examine the church accounts. However, they can only work with the procedure record they are given. For

the church auditing of accounts is carried out by the individual in accordance with proper procedure and Gift Aid and other tax regulations.

a. Ensure that all the receipts are acknowledged by and recorded according to their profile number. Monetary gifts should also be acknowledged and recorded accordingly. Details of each monetary transaction with the cross reference between the invoice and the cheque for each disbursement and also any backup paperwork with collections and bank deposit records must be documented appropriately.

b. All the cancelled receipts and cheques payable should be retained and duplicate sheets or cheques stubs endorsed appropriately.

9. Prepare an excellent annual statement of accounts. These should give as full information as possible. Layout should be clear. This is important that those who are not sure or used to working with accounts are not intimidated by the presentation of this information.

Financial Stewardship

This is not law, but what I believe are necessary for the Church's financial transactions, as a bishop. The Treasurer essentially serves as the Chief Financial Officer for the church. Specific responsibilities—which should be set forth in the church—include, but are not limited to:

- Maintaining accurate records of church finances
- Overseeing the receipt and recording of all income
- Overseeing the money and recording of all
- Performing or overseeing the recording of all members' gifts into personal giving records.
- Managing payment or working directly with a payroll company
- Preparing the monthly (or quarterly) financial reports for the Board of Directors
- Working with the Board of Directors to establish spending priorities
- Filing required tax forms (local, national, and international)

- Ensuring payment of monthly dues to Mount Calvary Church.
- Overseeing the counting and depositing of tithes and offerings
- Providing the congregation with any requested financial information
- Assisting in the preparation of the annual financial budget for the church.

Chronological List of Tasks for the Treasurer

- **Weekly/Bi-weekly**

1. Ensures that payroll information is submitted timely to the church if applicable.
2. Ensures that money checks are processed in accordance with the church's FOP.
3. Ensures that qualified counters are available each Sunday (and for every event in which an offering is collected).
4. Ensures that deposits are made or properly secured in accordance with FOP.

- **Monthly**

Ensure that bank statements are kept.

1. Ensure that an up to date analysis of the current financial position of the church is available for review at each Board meeting, including bank account balances, and detailed actual versus budgeted income/ expense analysis of the church.
2. Oversees the preparation and submission of the monthly Tithe and offering to the MCC.

- **Quarterly**

1. In the event that payroll is handled within the church, the Treasurer shall ensure the following items are completed in a timely basis:

a. Submits quarterly withholding taxes to the IRS or an approved agent

b. Submits quarterly NIS report to the IRS of payroll and deductions

• Annually

1. Develops or works in conjunction with a budget committee to develop the proposed operating fund budget for submission to the Board and approval by the congregation.

2. Oversees preparation of financial reports for presentation at congregational meetings and forums.

3. In the event that payroll is handled within the church, the Treasurer shall ensure the following items are completed in a timely basis:

   a. Submits statement and/or pay applicable sales tax to the local jurisdiction, for any items sold during the year, in accordance with the jurisdiction's time frames.

   b. Ensures that annual gifts are provided to all donors in accordance with the church's FOP.

   c. Ensures that bank files are updated to be in alignment with current Board membership.

   d. Arranges for church financial records and practices review.

   e. Prepares financial statements (per instructions) for annual submission to MCC local, national international Headquarters Office.

• Regularly

1. In the event that payroll is handled within the church, the Treasurer shall ensure the following items are completed in a timely basis:

   a. Processing of payroll payments.

   b. Ensures that all files for each employee are well kept for tax withholding purposes.

2. Conducts official business with the church's financial institution(s).

3. Maintains a positive working relationship with the Bookkeeper, if applicable.

The stewardship recorder receives information with a clear audit trail. Example, Gift Aid regulations and any other requirements will be strictly adhered to. It is important that the church congregation feels comfortable and secure that their gifts are being recorded appropriately and confidentially. If there are any restrictions on the use of the gift, these must be notified to the treasurer to ensure that they are adhered to and shown correctly in the accounting records.

I believe that in these cases that the envelopes or other records of the giver's intentions can be retained as appropriate. They are an official source of documentation required by the tax authorities and should be kept on file by date, and cross referenced by the giver. Records should be kept in a lockable storage area.

1. It is essential to send each donor an annual itemised statement giving a summary of all donations made during the previous tax year. These are required by donors for their own information and tax purposes. This can be done in the form of an annual thank you letter.

2. Report at the annual church the total amounts pledged and the total amounts received for the year together with other appropriate information.

3. Keep accurate records and documentation of all gifts in accordance with government regulations {Gift Aid}, Charities Commission Regulations, and your church requirements.

Duties and responsibilities

This is intended as a guide to the responsibilities of the different jobs, which make up the financial management of the local, national or international church. It is recognised that in some churches these jobs may be combined. It does not require him or her personally to do all the individual tasks, but where something is delegated, it remains the treasurer's responsibility to ensure that the activity is being done properly.

1. Ensure that the attention is directed to the statement in your church manual. These include the official denominational statements of the responsibilities and duties of the treasurer of the local church, and are the basis for all material appearing hereinafter.

2. Ensure that Non church funds are not mixed with Church funds. It is not advisable for the church Treasurer to become involved as the custodian of funds not properly a part of the authorized local church programme. In fact, in no case should funds not belonging to the church or to church sponsored organisations, appear on the records of the church Treasurers. Independent ministries—donors giving to other than denominational programmes, should be advised to send their donations direct rather than through the church treasury. The reason being the independent ministries are not audited. The church must protect its tax exempt status.

3. Church bank account

   a. Name and Authorization: All funds of the church are to be deposited promptly and kept on deposit in a bank account maintained in the name of the church (not in the name of the treasurer or any minister). Designation of the bank shall be made by action of the church board, and authorization of signatures for withdrawal of funds is also by specific church board action.

   b. Designation of Signatories: It is customary to authorise two or three signatures on the church bank account: that of the church secretary, treasurer or chairperson of finance committee and the minister. It is essential that two individuals are authorised to sign. In no case should only one person sign. Cheques should never be signed in blank, therefore it is practical to have at least four signatories.

   c. Change in Signature: Changes are made by individual name, not by designation of position. And prompt response to authorise action to withdraw the authorization is essential. And any change in signature shall be promptly communicated to the bank by the church chairperson or minister.

Responsibilities and Duties

General

- Have a love of God and demonstrate a commitment to following the way of Christ.

- Be knowledgeable or obtain knowledge about church finance and accountability.

- Oversee and account for assets and liabilities, according to decisions of the congregation, Board and Denomination, in a reasonable, ethical and legal manner.

Weekly/Semi-Monthly

- Supervise collection, counting and deposit of contributions; ensuring at least two persons are present during collection and counting.

- Supervise timely payment of ordinary operating expenditures, including payroll. For irregular or non-operating expenditures, obtain permission or approval of the appropriate authority.

- Supervise and/or post transactions to the church ledger or provide for same.

Monthly

- Attend Board Meetings.

- Reconcile bank account statements to church ledger.

- Maintain records of all income, revenue, receipts, expenses, disbursements, assets and liabilities, especially documents related to loans, mortgages, investments and payroll taxes.

- Provide financial reports to the Board and Denomination on operating funds, non-operating funds, and cash balances / investments.

- Provide a summary of financial reports for the bulletin and/or newsletter.

Quarterly

- Provide a statement of giving to contributors following appropriate IRS regulations for tax deductibility.

- Prepare and report tax information, meeting IRS requirements.

- Supervise treasurers of all other congregational accounts, ensuring they follow appropriate procedures and safeguards.

Annually

- Arrange for an audit/review of financial records and processes, sending a copy of results to Mount Calvary Church {MCC}.

- Oversee the financial planning including preparation of the annual budget.

- Ensure the preparation of financial sections of the Annual Report.

- Ensure the preparation of the yearend tax information including 1099-Misc and W-2 forms.

- Ensure processing of the commitments to the annual giving campaign or other campaigns of the congregation.

- Provide a detailed financial report for all Congregational Meetings.

- Report to the Denominational Pension Fund any changes in minister's compensation. The arrival or departure of minister should also be reported.

General Ledger/Personnel:

___Medical Insurance

___Honorariums

___Professional Dues & Subscriptions

___Pension (MCC)

___Workers Compensation Insurance

General Ledger/Administration:

___Pastor / Board Discretionary

___Permits and Fees

___Software Support (ACS)

___Ministry Support

___Office Supplies

___Postage

___Copier

General Ledger/Ministry:

___Communication

___Congregational Care

___Worship & Celebration

___Children & Youth

___Education and Enrichment

___Teaching Church

___Music

___Social & Fellowship

___Welcome Team

Restricted Funds:

___Benevolence

___Building

___Christian Social Action

___Conference

___Pastor's Education

___Building Maintenance

___Equipment

___Tithe (MCC)

Restricted Funds (DONOR):

___Donor Restricted Fund

___DR Ground Spring

Obligated Funds:

___Love Offering

___Retreat

___Flowers

___Special Events

___Education Events

___Musical Concerts / Events

Contributor

I commend this Ministerial Book as a tool for ministry and as another Biblical Resource for understanding the Ministries from within the context of Church life in a time such as this. The author of this book: "Practical Policy Making and Job Description in Christian Ministry and Mission", is a leader of leaders and a gifted teacher. I believe that Bishop Allan writes from a Biblical perspective that is not only sound but needed for times where diversity can sometimes get in the way of Biblical basics of understanding what ministry in the Lord's Church is all about.

I thank the Lord for Bishop Allan P Miller and his contagious enthusiasm for seeing the people of God becoming effective and equipped for the work of God and His Kingdom.

Tony Burford, BA, MA.,

Vicar, St John and St Matthew's Church

Deanery of Havering, Episcopal Area of Barking

Diocese of Chelmsford, Church of England

Chapter Ten

The Ministry of the Trustee Board

Financial Matters

Ministry is something that God does through the church before it is anything we do. Our significance, as leaders, is responsive. We are here, in different areas of leadership of God's people, because we have responded to a summons, because we were sought, called, sent and commissioned by one greater than ourselves that our lives might be expended in work more significant than ourselves. In those moments, our only hope is to know that God has a plan and purpose for how our meagre efforts fit into His larger scheme of things.

In a culture of omnivorous need, all-consuming narcissism, trustees who have no more compelling motive for their church ministry than 'meeting people's needs' are dangerous to themselves and to a church ministry that lacks a clear sense of who it is. We must be called and recalled to take on this ministry role as trustee of being grasped by something greater than ourselves, namely our trustee board to speak and to enact the Word of God among God's people. An essential role of the Trustee board is to meet and endorse the Church's budget when must have been prepared in the last quarter of the preceding year. This will usually be drafted by the finance committee / trustee. In order for this board to take financial responsibility and decisions it must receive regular, understandable, financial reports—preferably at least quarterly.

Membership of the Trustee Board should not be based on natural qualities or secular skills alone; they must be spiritual men, men of faith, wisdom and positive and credible character. The Apostles put forth the following pre-requisites for Deacons, which may be sued for Trustee Board Membership.

Therefore, brethren, look ye out among you seven men of honest report, full of the Holy Ghost and wisdom, whom we may appoint over this business {Acts 6:3 AV}.

The trustee should ensure that Church budget is implement according to plan. A full report should show 'actual' against 'budget' and against 'the same time last year'. They should also show outstanding liabilities and the current balances on bank and other account split into the various funds. Any variance from 10 percent or more against budget or a large amount should be fully explained.

Jesus understood that true life-transformation is more about asking the right questions rather than about always giving the correct answers. Church is not dealing with the hard questions. For many, the church is not a safe space to ask honest life questions for fear of harsh judgment and criticism. Trustee in this new era must make room for tough questions and trust the Spirit of God to change people's lives. I guess I'm what you consider a seeker. All along I've tried to translate things Christian people say into meanings that I can embrace. It seems to work for me. The annual report and Accounts should be presented to the local church by the Treasurer for agreement prior to the A G Meeting of the church. If the Independent Examiner {IE} / Auditor cannot give an unconditional report the local church must obtain adequate explanations regarding their concerns.

Men and women of every conceivable strength and capability are found giving effective leadership in churches and ministries around the globe. But the diversity of gifts does not lessen the necessity for leadership in the church ministry. Whatever the gifts, interests or abilities of the trustee board members are vital components of the work of every ministry. So the minister and the church board should be satisfied that the Independent Examiner / Auditor is suitable in terms of qualifications and in relationship to the treasurer. It is important that someone other than the Treasurer has at least met the Independent Examiner {IE} or Auditor.

Insurance

It requires careful attention to the delicate balance that must often be struck between the variety of pressures that are at work in the leadership and trustee board environment. It is the responsibility of the church board to ensure that the church has appropriate insurance. Insurance arrangements and levels of cover should be reviewed regularly. Various companies which specialise in church insurance and other major companies will provide quotes. Public Liability Insurance is compulsory and the building{s} and contents should be insured as well. The church may also need insurance as an employer and cover accidents to volunteers. If cash or other church property is taken off the premises this will also need to be covered. It is also important to include computer data. Insurance companies now restrict cover for damage from terrorist actions to £100,000. It will be for the church board to decide whether extra cover, which is relatively expensive, is appropriate.

Tax

The wise leader will always be attentive to the threats inherent in facilitating change in the local, national and international church. He or she must develop a high degree of tolerance for the processes necessary to effect change, stabilise the changes made and prepare the church for the next level of change toward the fulfilment of the goals of the church ministry. A registered church can benefit in a number of ways, especially in relation to tax issues. The church which is a charity which is exempt from registration with the Charity Commissioner and does not therefore have a charity number, will have an identifying number {beginning with an x} from the Inland Revenue {IR}. The IR require anyone dealing with the tax affairs, particularly tax claims, to be authorised. There is a specific Inland Revenue form for this.

It is the willingness and the ability to carefully steward the resources of the church ministry towards the fulfilment of its mission. It is the stewardship of this trustee board, the values and the legacy of the church ministry, and its focus is found in relationships. These members are the heart and spirit of the leadership endeavour. Conceptions of power and privilege are out of place in church leadership, antithetical to its purposes, and destructive of the ethos out of which the church ministry derives its identity as the Body of Christ, the community of faith. It is essential for the Church to comply with existing laws or regulations in their communities. The Church through its leaderships needs to comply with PAYE / National Insurance legislation as well as all other employment legislation including Health and Safety, Working time Regulations and Stakeholder Pension legislation.

Church administration is a leadership function and consists of the organisation of the people and the resources of the church for the accomplishment of the objectives of the kingdom of God. It cannot be done unilaterally. It is, by the very nature of the task, highly relational in its pursuit. This task consists, however, in discovering, unleashing and polishing the variety of gifts that people bring to a trustee board of church ministry so that they may work together in a harmonious whole to 'get the job done'. One can get more information about employing staff from a good Finance Adviser.

The mission of the church ministry is not a solo accomplishment by only one person but the group. The driven type personality so often epitomised as the ideal leader can easily become a liability in any volunteer organisation but especially in the church. It requires that a church recruits and coalesce a group of people into an effective and focused team, working together to accomplish their objectives. The relationships require someone knowledge to find out that some churches are not generally exempt from VAT. However, in most cases new building works will be exempt from VAT. If the church building is listed {grade I, II or III*} then it is possible to claim a grant which is equal to the cost of VAT on some repairs to the building.

The Mount Calvary Church:—like other churches is planning to engage in some profit making enterprises {e.g. a coffee shop, supermarket and bookshop also properties}. The Church is not exempt from paying Corporation Tax on the profit from these activities. If turnover, {not profit}, from the trading activity exceeds £5,000 per annum there may be a Corporation Tax liability and the church should or will seek advice from the Finance Adviser or a qualified Accountant. It is much more than the product of the inspiration given to anyone individual, especially in this church ministry. It is the product of the shared view of the leadership and those who are the frontline workers and organisers who carry the vision forward.

The nature of the church is expressed in community. It is not a one-man show. It is the gathering up of the gifts, abilities and vision of the whole, inspired by the Holy Spirit and brought to focus and passion through the gifts and passion of a minister. According to the Charity Commission regulations, churches that are registered with the Charity Commission can claim back tax on Gift Aid donations and bank interest can be paid without deduction of tax on completion of a form provided by the relevant bank.

Risk Management Audit that Mount Calvary Church will be using

The following risk management audit has been designed to help churches in effective Church management. It is designed and adopted by our Church—Mount Calvary Church—and I believe it will be useful to other churches and ministries.

Employment Paid and Volunteer	Yes	No	Don't Know	Comment
Does each Minister (paid or volunteer) who is doing an active, authorized and accountable ministry in your church have a current employment contract / covenant?				
Do you have a sexual harassment policy?				
Have background checks been done on all persons (paid or volunteer) who are involved in children, youth or counselling ministries?				
Do you have personnel policies concerning the handling of employee records that address the privacy issues involved?				

Financial Management	Yes	No	Don't Know	Comment
Are all signature authorities reviewed and updated at least annually and are all checks and other bank instructions signed by two signatories?				
Are at least two persons present during the counting of church offerings and are these persons rotated periodically?				
Are offerings promptly deposited in a church bank account?				
Are monthly bank statements reconciled with recorded income and expenses?				
Are monthly written financial reports provided promptly to Board members?				
Does the congregation approve your annual budget prior to the beginning of the new financial year?				
Does the Board keep to the budget approved by the congregation and is there a procedure in place for reporting exceptions?				
Do you comply with all donor restrictions on designated contributions?				

	Yes	No	Don't Know	Comment
Do you have personnel policies approved by the Board to promptly and thoroughly investigate allegations of misconduct by church workers or employees?				

Employment Paid and Volunteer	Yes	No	Don't Know	Comment
Do you adequately orient new employees / volunteers concerning employer policies and procedures?				
What ongoing training is provided by church employees/volunteers to help them perform their duties in light of changing national and local laws?				
Are all employees and volunteers supervised to reduce their risk of negligence and misconduct?				
Does the church issue the appropriate Internal Revenue Service forms to all church staff and others who have been receiving financial compensation from the church during the previous year?				

Insurance	Yes	No	Don't Know	comment
Do you provide Worker's Compensation Insurance for all paid staff?				
Do you have general liability insurance with minimum coverage of £1 million and director's insurance? Please submit a copy of the declaration page indicating the amounts.				
Do you annually review your insurance policies and other possible coverage and is this documented in your Board of Trustees minutes?				
Do you have proper documentation of church assets?				
Do you contact your insurance agent as soon as a loss occurs or an allegation of negligence or misconduct is made?				
Do you comply with all conditions specified in your insurance policies?				

Church Records	Yes	No	Don't Know	Comment
Do you have a copy of your bylaws kept in a safe place outside of the church/pastor's office?				
Is your church incorporated?				
Have you filed all annual reports required by the government?				
Have all changes to your bylaws been approved by the Network Ministers?				
Do you have a records retention policy that specifies how long church records are to be kept?				
Are legal documents such as Board of Trustees Meetings Minutes and Congregational Meeting Minutes kept readily available?				
Where do you maintain your important legal records such as deeds, rent agreements, etc.?				
Are Minutes and financial reports posted so that church members can view them?				

Copyright and Publications	Yes	No	Don't Know	Comment
Do you have a license that allows you to reproduce music? (i.e., CCLI license)				
Do you include proper citations in your bulletin and other written materials when copyrighted materials are used?				
Do you have a license that allows you to legally copy and share commercial recordings of songs the choirs want to learn? (i.e. Rehearsal license from CCLI)				
Do you have a license that allows you to stream or podcast your live-recorded worship music on your church's website or other streaming service? (CCLI Church Streaming and broadcast License).				
Do you have a license that allows you to use movies for any ministry related activities? (i.e. CVLI Church Video License)				

Board of Directors	Yes	No	Don't Know	Comment
Do you adequately train new Board members?				
When was the most recent Board training?				
Do you provide ongoing training of Board members, including officers?				

If you are considering appointing someone to a paid position then the role might like to be formalised a bit further and the following job description / draft contract could be used as a guide. Many parts of it will depend on the size of the ministry or church organization and the complexity of activities going on and will not be applicable to all.

Appointment

Your appointment will run from ... until ... We would request you giving at least ... months notices of your intention to leave the position. We would expect the post to take up ... day / hours per week with the times to be engaged in these duties by mutual agreement. We would expect you to attend ... church meetings, standing committee meetings and other meetings as part of your role. You will be paid £ ... per annum / month, reviewable annually.

a. It cannot be overemphasized to strongly recommend that the church Treasurer is acting in a position of sacred trust, both as to the church members whose contributions he or she receives and as to the various options church organisations for whose benefits these funds are administered. In discharging this responsibility, the following points should be kept in order:

b. Conferences funds. All tithes and all funds for the world mission programme, as well as special project funds administered by the local, national, regional destinations, are designated on the church Treasurers book as conference funds. Such funds are never to be used for local church needs, but are held in trust by the church Treasurers, and are remitted in full to the local conference treasurer by the approved date of each month.

c. Local church funds. This classification includes all funds received for the local church expenses, building and repair funds, local church missionary and poor funds, training and development expenses, and the specific funds of local church programmes, such as the community services, etc. These funds should be dispatched separately by the church Treasurers only on the authorization of the board or committee designated as to control them in each case.

d. Overdraft. It is evident that if any particular fund is permitted to become overdrawn, some other designated recipient funds must have been used, with the authority of the board, to cover such overdraft. Such a situation constitutes a breach of trust by the church Treasurers, in permitting funds in his or her care to be used for any reason.

5. Payment by church members. It is an essential and a regular practice for Church members to place their tithes and offerings in envelopes provided. And timely preparation and making of bank deposits, is carried out by the cashier under the responsibility of the church board in accordance with proper procedure.

a. Receipts for base principles. While various types of receipting systems have been authorised to receive the needs of the local churches from the smallest to the largest, all are based on the principle that the church Treasurer writes a good receipt for all funds passing into his or her custody, whatever their source, immediately at the time he or she receives the money.

6. Weekly church offering

a. Designation of purpose of offering. It is a customary principle in our churches to assign the offering taken at the church services to a specific purpose. And no lest then two people should count offering collections {Cash and envelopes} as soon as possible. The people should not be related to each other, not be the same two each week and not always include the treasurer. The income details should be recorded in the service register and initialled by the counters. Some of these purposes are designed by Bishop Allan Miller at the setup of the church. Others are designated by the way the local ministry itself operates, such as offering for the local church budget, for the church outreach, etc.

b. Money should be banked as soon as possible and left in the safe until it is banked. If it is necessary to take money home prior to banking, ensure it is covered by your home insurance.

Keep these Responsibilities in mind:

- Process all checks, recording them in the appropriate accounting software program.

- Process all payroll checks, Tax Form 941's, W-2's and other government records required in a timely fashion.

- Insure that computer files are backed up weekly, at a minimum monthly, and the back-ups are stored off premises.

- Prepare the monthly and annual finance report.

- Supervise daily cash balances to insure sufficient funds are maintained.

- Maintain filing system and storage system for all financial records and banking records for easy retrieval.

- Prepare records for annual audit

- Maintain historical data, and establish a retention system for old financial records in accordance with government requirements (minimum of 5 years).

- File all the required federal, state, and local tax forms.

- Assist in the preparation of the annual budget.

Contributor

Apostolic leadership, by its calling, has great responsibility. And as such, much is expected of leaders {See: Luke 12:48}. In the modern world, in most cases, it is much easier for older, more established and more stable churches and ministries to succeed than young and struggling churches. Whether a Christian leader uses the title or not, we have to remember that the most important attribute of any leader in the kingdom of Christ Jesus is to have the attitude of a servant. The author, Dr. Allan Miller, has laid out simple workable and practical guidelines, with lots of valuable information to help churches to succeed and grow strong. His teaching in this book is what I call "Apostolic Truth", which is a fanciful way of explaining what apostolic teaching is.

We should bear in mind that Apostolic Truth is not mere theological facts or philosophical concepts. But is truth based on the principles taught in the Word of God, the "foundation of the Apostles" upon which we must all build. Dr. Allan Miller has written this book not only from his depth of biblical and theological knowledge, but also from his vast experience in ministry—both as a minister and teacher of ministers. His covers several areas of ministry which I believe will be useful for the Church.

I wholeheartedly identify—and totally recommend—the principles of financial management set forth by Dr. Miller in this book. This book will help the Church to understand how to handle people's funds and comply with the established laws relating to Church funds and charity. Thus ministers can avoid the temptations connected with mismanagement or misappropriation of Church money.

Dr. Miller, has done a great work and I congratulate him for his efforts and achievement.

H John, D. Min., PhD.

Professor in Biblical Preaching and Church Leadership

Chapter Eleven

The Ministry of Deacons and Deaconesses

The Meaning of Deacon

The word "Deacon" is from the Greek word DIAKONOS, which primarily denotes "a servant", "whether as doing servile work, or as an attendant rendering free service, without particular reference to its character".[3] The word is used in the New Testament in reference to:

1. Domestic servants (John 2:5, 9).

2. The civil rulers (Romans 13:4).

3. Christ Himself (Romans 15:8; Gal.2:17).

4. The ministers of Christ in relation to their Lord, as Master (John 12:26; Eph.6:21; Col.1:7; 4:7).

5. The Disciples of Christ in relation to one another (Matt.20:26; 23:11; Mark 9:35; 10:43).

6. The servants of Christ in the work of preaching and teaching (1Cor.3:5; 2 Cor.3:6; 6:4; 11:23; Eph.3:7; Col.1:23, 25).

7. Those who serve in the churches are known as "Servants" or "Deacons" of the churches (Rom.16:1).

8. Servants of Satan—as false apostles or false ministers (2 Cor.11:15).

The word "Deacon" is also mentioned in the New Testament as an official or worker in the local Church (See: Phil.1:1; 1 Tim.3:8-13). As explained earlier, the Greek word used for Deacon simply means a servant or an

3 W. E. Vine, Vine's Concise Dictionary of the Bible Words, Nashville: Thomas Nelson Publishers, 1999, p.82

attendant, especially in menial work. The word is borrowed from the secular concept of servant-hood and used in the Church, in reference to those who "serve" in a menial capacity. The word appears in two passages (Phil.1:1 and 1 Tim.3:8-13) and it is used in reference to a woman, as "a servant of the Church" (Rom.16:1).

The Orgin of Deacons in the Church

The office of deacons originated in the Church in Jerusalem, resulting from some internal, racial or cultural and administrative problems in the Church. There was a complaint from the Hellenistic (Greek speaking) Christians against the Hebrews (Jewish Christians) over the neglect of their widows.

And in those days, when the number of the disciples was multiplied, there arose a murmuring of the Grecians against the Hebrews, because their widows were neglected in the daily ministration (Acts 6:1 AV).

As the Church multiplied in number, so did the needs of the people increased. But the Apostles had not considered the need to delegate responsibilities to Church members. The twelve men who governed the Church, when the membership was 120 ((Acts 1:14), still governed the Church when the membership was over 5,000 (Acts 2:41; 4:4). They were virtually in charge of every ministry in the Church—both the menial or not too spiritual and the spiritual.

Thus, by combining the "daily ministration" of food stuff and material things to the widows and "serving tables" with their personal devotion and preaching ministry, the apostles became totally ineffective in both areas of ministry. This must have had a toll on their physical, emotional and spiritual well being. This is usually the case when leaders work too hard, in a growing ministry, without delegating responsibilities (See the example of Moses in Exodus 18:13-26).

To solve these problems, the apostles wisely suggested that seven men be chosen from the Church, whom they might appoint "to serve tables" (Acts 6:2) or "over this business" (Acts 6:3)—the business of the distribution of funds—so that they might be able to devote more of their time to prayer and the spiritual needs of the Church.

Then the twelve called the multitude of the disciples unto them, and said, it is not reason that we should leave the word of God and serve tables. Wherefore, brethren, look ye out among you seven men of honest report, full of the Holy Ghost and wisdom, whom we may appoint over this business. But we will give ourselves continually to prayer, and to the ministry of the word (Acts 6:2-4 AV).

The Greek word used here for "serve" (Acts 6:2) is diakoneo, which means "to serve", "to await upon" or "to attend to". It is from the same root with the word used for Deacon, which clearly defines the function of a Deacon in the Church—that is to serve; thus a deacon is a "servant", one who serves. It is the same word used in relation to Martha, who "served" her guests at the table (Luke 10:40; John 12:2).

The first Deacons were appointed as officers or servants, to attend to the secular (or non-spiritual) matters of the Church—so that the apostles might give more of their time to private study, prayer and the ministry of the Word. Thus, the deacon played a subordinate role, not in the regular preaching or pulpit ministry, but in menial and administrative functions as well ministering to the material needs of the Church members.

Deaconess

"Deaconess" is a female Church official who does the work of a deacon. Though the word "deaconess" is not directly mentioned in the New Testament, the Bible makes reference to several individuals who served as deaconesses in the Church.

In Romans 16:1, Paul wrote: I commend unto you Phebe our sister, which is a servant of the Church which is at Cenchrea (Romans 16:1 AV).

The Greek word used here for "servant", DIAKONOS, is the same word used for deacons in Phil.1:1; 1 Tim.3:8, 12. It is used here in reference to "Phebe our sister", who was a Deanconess or a female deacon at the Church in Cenchrea. In the same chapter, Paul mentioned certain women who may be described as deaconesses. They includes:

a. Mary "who bestowed much labour (Greek KOPIAO—to work hard) on us (verse 6).

b. Tryphena, "who laboured (Greek KOPIAO) in the Lord" (verse 12)

c. Persia (meaning a Persian woman) who "laboured (Greek KOPIAO) much in the Lord" (verse 12).

In 1 Corinthians 16:15-16, Paul referred to a sister called "Stephanas", one of his first converts in Achia, who was devoted to "the ministry of the saints" (1 Cor.16:15). The Greek word used here for "ministry" is DIAKONIA, which means "attendance", "service" or to serve as a deacon (Greek DIA-KONOS). The same word used here for "ministry" is used as "ministration" in Acts 6:1, "daily ministration" of the distribution of funds, food stuffs and the welfare of widows.

Thus "Ministry to the Saints", is simply "rendering service to the saints" or "attending to the needs of the saints". It is therefore not to be viewed as a regular pulpit ministry, but of taking care of the welfare or material needs of the saints. Paul urged the saints to "submit yourselves unto such", since they were delegated Church officials (1 Cor.16:16). In verse 17, Paul described the specific "ministry to the saints" of Stephanas, including Fortunatus and Achaicus, "for that which was lacking on your part they have supplied". This could mean financial assistance or helping to supply the material needs of Paul or attending to his need or welfare. (See examples of such women's ministry—Exod.35:25; Luke 8:2-3; Acts 9:39).

Joanna, the wife of Chuza, Herod's stewards, and Susanna, and several other women "ministered unto Christ of their substance" (Luke 8:3). The Greek word used here for "ministered", is DIAKONEO, which means "to attend to", "to wait upon (menially or as a host)", to aid or relief. It is the same Greek word translated Deacon in 1 Tim.3:10, 13. These women did to Christ the work expected of deaconesses in the Church. Other women who "ministered" (as deaconesses) to Christ, included, "Mary Magdalene, Mary the mother of James, the less and of Joses, and Salome ... and many other women" Mark 15:40-41).

In the Pastorals certain women are indirectly described as deaconesses:

a. **In 1 Tim.3:10-11**, in direct reference to deacons, Paul said, "even so must their wives be grave" (verse 11). Some scholars believe that the "wives" here must either be "wives of deacons" or "women deacons". This is based on the Greek word translated "wives", which is also translated "women" in other places. The Greek word GUNE, which is translated "wives" (in Acts 21:5; 1 Cor.7:29; Eph.5:22, 24, 25, 28; Col.3:18-19; 1 Tim.3:11; 1 Pet.3:1) is also translated "women" (in Matt.11:11; 14:21; 15:38; 27:55; Mark 15:40, 41; Luke 1:28, 42; 7:28; 8:2; 17:35; 23:27, 49, 55;24:10, 22, 24; Acts 1:14; 5:14; 8:3, 12; 9:2; 13:50; 16:13; 17:4, 12; 22:4; 1 Cor.14:34,35; 1 Tim.2:9,10; Heb.11:35; 1 pet.3:5; Rev.9:8; 14:4). Although the text favours "wives of deacons" or "deacons' wives", some scholars claim that it can be used either as "wives of deacons" or "women (female) deacons" (deaconesses) or "wives of pastors" or women Church workers in general.

b. **In 1 Tim.5,** Paul distinguished between "elderly women" (1 Tim.5:2) and "young women" (1 Tim.5:2) and "widows indeed" (elderly widows—verse 3) and younger widows (verse 11). While the elderly widows should be considered to serve in the Church (verses 3-10), younger widows should be encouraged to remarry and not be considered for full time ministry work (verses 11-14). We understand that these elderly widows are to serve as "deaconesses" in the Church and to be taken care of by the Church, except they have relatives who can take care of them. While not all elderly people should be involved in Church ministry (the elderly mentioned in verses 1-2 are aged people, not necessarily "Church Elders" or officials), some elderly women (and men) can be very useful in ministry, as deacons and deaconesses. Their wealth of experience, maturity, wisdom and spirituality can be great assets to the Church.

c. **In Titus 2:3-5,** these aged members of the Christian community, who serve as deaconesses, have responsibilities towards younger women (and their children). As deaconesses, they should teach young women:

d. To be sober verse 4 (Greek: SOPHRONIZO, "to cause to be of sound mind", to cultivate sound judgment, to be disciplined).

e. To love their husbands (verse 4).

f. To love their children (verse 4).

g. To be discreet (verse 5).

h. To be chaste (verse 5).

i. To be good keepers of their homes (verse 5)

j. To be good (of good behaviour)—verse 5

k. To be obedient to their own husbands (verse 5).

In Philip 4:3, Paul made reference to certain women who assisted him in the gospel ministry. Paul wrote to the Church to "help those women which laboured with me in the gospel" (Phil.4:3). The Greek word used here for "laboured", is SUNATHLEO, which means "striving together" (as in Phil.1:27), to wrestle in company with, to contend at ones side. These women may have been engaged in a ceaseless prayer warfare or intercessory ministry on behalf of the Apostle Paul. We can "strive together in prayer" (Rom.15:30), on behalf of Church leaders, to make their ministry effective. This is also a significant function of deaconesses, especially those gifted as prayer warriors. We may also include sister Dorcas, the Church in Joppa (Acts 9:36-42) and sister Lydia, whose house became a place of worship (Acts 16:14-15, 40) as good examples of deaconesses.

Qualifications of Deacons

We recommend that any worker to be appointed for the office of a deacon must be a regenerated, matured and experienced Christian. He must have been a Born Again Christian for not less than five years, and must have been a member of our Church for not less than two years (unless in very exceptional cases or by the leading of the Holy Spirit). In addition to the above, a deacon must possess the following essential pre-requisites:

According to Acts 6:3-8:

1. Must have honest report (verse 3)

2. Must be full of the Holy Ghost (verse 3)

3. Must be a wise man (verse 3)

4. Must have the ability / willingness to serve as delegated by the leadership (verses 3, 10).

5. Ability to handle Church business affairs (not all deacons are good administrators—some are better for the administrative functions of the Church)—verse 3.

6. Must be a man of faith (verses 5, 8).

According to 1Timothy 3:8-13:

7. Must be grave (Greek: SEMNOS—honourable, venerable; 1 Tim.3:8; See also: 1 Tim.3:11; Tit.2:2).

8. Not double tongued (1 Tim.3:8).

9. Not given to much wine—not a drink and (1 Tim.3:8).

10. Not greedy of filthy lucre—not money minded (1 Tim.3:8).

11. Purity of conscience (1 Tim.3:8).

12. Must have experience—must have undergone a probationary period satisfactorily (1 Tim.3:10).

13. Must have a credible character / integrity—"must be blameless" (1 Tim.3:10).

14. Can be trusted to defend the gospel (cp.1 Tim.1:19; 3:9; Tit.1:9).

15. Married to only one wife (1 Tim.3:12).

16. A well-ordered domestic life. A good manager of his household (1 Tim.3:12; cp. 1 Tim.3:4-5; Tit.1:6).

17. Deacons who have served well and demonstrated some special abilities and gifts for ministry can be considered for promotion to a higher level of ministry (see: 1 Tim.3:13).

According to Titus 2:2

18. Must be sober (Greek: NEPHALEOS—circumspect, vigilant)

19. Temperate or self-controlled or self-disciplined.

20. Sound in faith

21. Sound in charity (love)

22. Sound in patience (or endurance).

According to Exodus 18:21

23. Deacons must be men of abilities or capabilities: "able men" (verse 21).

24. God-fearing men (verse 21).

25. Truthful men—with personal integrity (verse 21)

26. Not covetous—"hating covetousness"—that is, not money minded (verse 21).

In Addition:

27. Must be a faithful ambassador—of Christ and of the Church (Prov.13:17).

28. A faithful messenger (Prov.25:13) or faithful enough to be entrusted with Church responsibilities (2 Tim.2:2).

29. Must be a faithful steward in the Church (1 Cor.4:1-2).

Qualifications for Deaconess

In addition to what have been said about the spiritual qualifications of deacons, deaconesses must possess these qualities.

1. Must be grave—honourable, respectable, venerable—(1 Tim.3:11).

2. Must not be slanderers (1 Tim. 3:11) Greek: DIABOLOS—devil, false accusers, like Jezebel or Potiphar's wife.

3. Must be sober (1 Tim.3:11(Greek: NEPHALEOS—circumspect, vigilant).

4. Faithful in all things (1 Tim.3:11)—faithful to God, to their husbands and to the church.

5. They must practice modesty—especially in talking, behaviour and appearance (1 Tim.2:9-10; See also: Pro.31:25; 1 Pet.3:1-2).

6. A deaconesses must not be a domineering woman. She should be submissive to male leaders in the Church and their husbands at home (1 Tim.2:9-10; cp.1 Pet.3:1-6).

7. She must be a virtuous woman (Prov.12:14; 31:10, 29).

8. She must be a gracious woman (Prov.11:16).

9. A good builder—not a destroyer; a pillar, not a caterpillar (Prov.14:1).

10. She must have wisdom, good discretion or prudence (Prov.31:26; cp. Tit.2:5).

11. A deaconesses must be hospitable (2 Kings 4: 10; Acts 16:14, 15, 40).

12. She must be discerning or a good sense of judgment (2 Kings 4:8-9).

13. She must be thoughtful (2 Kings 4:10).

14. The wife of only one husband—not a divorced and remarried—only a widow can remarry (Rom.7:1-3; 1 Cor.7:39).

15. Willingness to serve in menial duties—(John 12:2), willing to attend to guests at tables.

16. Not a stingy woman—but a good giver (Exod.35:25; Prov.31:20; Luke 8:2-3; 21:2-4; 1 Cor.15-16).

17. Positive in utterances (2 kings 4:23, 26).

18. Must have a well ordered domestic life; a good manageress of her domestic life, having respect for her husband, with well brought up children (Prov.31:23; 1 Tim.5:10; 1 Pet.3:1-6).

19. She must live a life governed by the fear of God (Pro.31:30).

20. She must have a good report—that is a good commendation (Pro.31:30-31; Mark 14:6; Acts 9:36-43; 1 Tim.5:10).

21. She must be a diligent woman (Prov.31:18-19).

22. She must be exemplarily punctual (Prov.31:15).

23. She must maintain a holy lifestyle (Tit.2:2).

24. She must be "a teacher of good things", in her ministry towards the younger female members of the Church (Tit.2:2).

25. She must not be a drinker of (or addicted to) alcoholic beverages (Tit.2:3).

26. A deaconesses must be disciplined in her utterances in public; she must be able to keep secrets, within the Christian community.

DUTIES OF DEACONS

The primary duty of deacons and deaconesses is to "SERVE". Their responsibilities in the early Church were basically "secular" in nature, though sacred in God's sight (for every ministry) in the Church, whether menial (welfare, visitation, ushering, clerical or administration) or spiritual (teaching, preaching, praying etc) should be conducted with the same motive, "as unto the Lord". Thus, their role is basically to "help" or "serve" in a subordinate capacity, as may be delegated by the leadership of the Church. While some deacons may preach, if they are so gifted or empowered, this is not their primary responsibility.

Their duties in the local Church include:

1. Deacons are usually "appointed" to manage the "business" aspect of the Church (Acts 6:4). This includes the administrative and.

2. To take care of the Church finances (as ushers/ or treasurers). To make sure that offering are well counted, recorded and banked.

3. Deacon (not all deacons) can serve as a member of the Church Board (or Trustee member).

4. Deacons can be appointed to take charge of the technical, electronics, mechanical and all equipment used for worship etc.

5. A deacon can be appointed as "officer in charge of sanitation"; he is to ensure that the Church (and premises) are kept in a clean and healthy condition in readiness for worship and after service.

6. In some churches, a deacon may be appointed as the Building Administrator, whose primary duty is to raise funds for building projects.

7. In some Pentecostal Churches, where there are no elders or assistant Pastors, deacons are delegated to assist the Pastors during Water Baptism and Holy Communion Service (this is common in the Baptist Churches).

8. A deacon can be a Sunday School Teacher / can be a Superintendent.

9. Deacons should be appointed to be in charge of Church vehicles and to convey Church members and Sunday school children to and from Church.

10. A deacon can serve as the personal assistant to the pastor.

11. Deacons can be appointed to head the welfare and charity departments of the Church.

This includes:

    a. Raising of funds for the poor.

    b. Distribution of food stuff to needy members.

    c. Taking care of helpless widows and unemployed Church members.

12. Deacons who possess certain abilities or spiritual gifts should be encouraged to exercise their gifts from time to time. They may be regularly appointed to:

    a. Give words of exhortation.

    b. To lead the Church in worship.

    c. To make announcements.

    d. To great the Church from time to time.

    e. To lead in prayer meetings.

    f. To read the Scriptures during Church service.

Senior Deacons

In the absence of Elders, the most senior or experienced among the deacons can serve in a supervisory capacity among the deacons. Such deacons should be directly accountable to the senior.

Such deacons who have served well and proved themselves to be faithful and trustworthy can be elevated (1 Tim.3:10). They may be delegated to head some departments of the Church. Some deacons are spiritually gifted in other areas of ministry; they can be teachers or preachers as well. Of the seven first deacons appointed in the early Church, Stephen and Philp possessed some extraordinary gifts for ministry. Stephen became an Evangelist who witnessed boldly for the Lord. He was the first martyr of the early Church (Acts 7). Philip also became a missionary / Evangelist (Acts; and later he became a Pastor in Caesana (Acts 8:40; 21:8-9).

Contributor

The author of this book: "Practical Policy Making and Job Description in Christian Ministry and Mission", is a man whom God has called to teach God's Ministers and Church Leaders. Having read his previous books by Dr Allan Miller, I know his books are well researched, practical and relevant.

This book spelled out the different types of leadership roles. Usually the human resources {personal} department of an organization of any size pick up a lot of this information. They would not have hired people in their present post or role unless they understood the needs. In the church ministry, however, it is easy to fall into that "willing worker syndrome" with no understanding.

Therefore, I am delighted to recommend his new book. It is actually concerning projected needs, long-range goals, and patterns of growth in their particular ministries.

Noel R. P. Taylor, BA. MA., D. Min.,

Senior Pastor, Gateway of Hope Christian Church

Islington: North London

Chapter Twelve

The Ministry of an Elder

The effective leader must utilise all the creative methodologies and approaches possible, consistent with the deeply held beliefs and values that brought the church ministry into existence. Creativity must be balanced with faithfulness. But careful leadership will recognise the opportunity to help the church ministry examine its purposes, its objectives and its faithfulness. He or she will not fear to help the church examine its methods but will see to it that in the examination, faithfulness to the character, values and beliefs of the church are reaffirmed, solidified and celebrated of the role of an elder.

The original government of the Hebrews was patriarchal, where the head of the family exercised the supreme rule over all of his descendants to the supreme head. Naturally only men of mature age came into these positions, hence the designation elder. He will understand that comfortable routines and methods that elders grow out of experience that is not always subject to objective evaluation. The elder methods are often deeply embedded in the self-identity of a church congregation, and opinions regarding their effectiveness will often take on spiritual dimensions.

The concept of "elder" is borrowed from the Old Testament political and tribal structures and its usage in Judaism. The Hebrew word "zaqen" is the usual word for "elder". It is used in reference to "an old man" or "old woman". It can refer to any person of old age, a person advanced in life. According to W. E. Vine, "The word zaqen has a more specialized use with the sense of "elder", a man, with gifts of leadership, wisdom, and justice; his duties varied to include religious, civic, and judicial activities, Josh.23:2; 1 Kings 12:8; Ezek. 8:1.[4]

In addition, the influence and functions of elders can be seen in the following:

1. Great influence of the older people of the nation.

2. Division of the Israelites into tribes, with a head, chief, or prince over each as a whole

3. General use, in other nations as well as among the Hebrews, the term "elder" is an official title for those who, as representatives of the people, made all their decisions.

The earliest mention of elders as a political body is at the time of the Exodus. The seventy elders mentioned in Exodus and Numbers were a sort of governing body, a parliament, and the origin of the tribunal of seventy elders called the "Sanhedrin" or "Council".

They were also, after the founding of the towns and cities, those who were put at the head of affairs who could not always derive authority from their position in the tribe. These were also called elders, and they served as judges, to decide both civil and criminal causes.

The roles and functions of elders in the pre-church era can be further explained as follows:

Elder with City

1. Elders of his city shall fetch Deut.19:12

2. Elders of that city shall take and Deut.21:3,6, 19; 22:15; 25:8

3. Declare his cause to elder Josh 20:4

4. Took the elder of the city Judges 8:16

5. Elders of every city Ezra 10:14, etc.

Elder of Israel

---

4 W. E.Vine, Vine's Concise Dictionary of the Bible Words, Nashville: Thomas Nelson Publisher, 1999, p.112

Develop an accountability relationship with someone who will reinforce your resolve to incorporate each of those purpose building activities into your life. If I reserve some time for interruptions, I review interruptions carefully to determine their value.

1. Gather elder of Israel together Ex. 3:16, 12:21, 17:5,
2. Elders of Israel came to eat with Ex. 18:12
3. Seventy of the elders of Israel Ex. 24:1,9
4. Elders of Israel commanded Deut.27:1, 31:9,
5. Rulers of people, elders of Israel Acts 4:8, etc

Elders with People

Our culture, with its hurried pace, pushes us to live in drive and overdrive. While we're very active and productive, fewer people have healthy relationships and God seems distant. No one cannot develop intimate, transparent relationships on the run. This is especially true of these elders. Clarify your specific purpose for each other life area or role. Here's a sample listing:

1. Called for elder of the people Ex. 19:7
2. To be elder of the people Num. 11:16
3. Before elder of my people 1 Sam. 15:30
4. The elders of the people came Matt. 21:23, Luke 22:66
5. Elder of the people took counsel Matt. 27:1 etc.

Elders in the Christian Church

The office of elder or presbyter was adopted into the Church from the Jewish synagogue; and the function of such was, in general, spiritual, but involved an oversight of all the affairs of the Church. As a rule the apostles never appointed persons as elders directly after they were converted. The elders were appointed and ordained by apostles and prophets to oversee and direct the affairs of the local churches established by the apostles.

The equivalent New Testament Word is the Greek adjective, "prcsbuteros", which denotes "an old man", an "elder". It is used for a person advanced in like, a senior. The feminine is used of "elder" women in the church; Paul wrote to Timothy, "Rebuke not an elder, but intreat him as a father ... the elder women as mothers ..." (1 Tim. 5:1-2). The word "elder" is used here in respect of age, not in respect of position or office. In the Christian Church, the word is used in respect of rank or office or leadership position.

According to Vine, "in the Christian churches those who, being raised up and qualified by the work of the Holy Spirit, were appointed to have the spiritual care of, and to exercise oversight over the churches. To these the term "bishops" ... or "overseers", is applied (see: Acts 20:17 with v.26, and Titus 1:5 and 7), the latter term indicating the nature of their work ... their maturity of spiritual experience ..."[5]

Ruling Elders

Elders were those who ruled or were appointed to leadership (1 Tim.5:17); these are clearly distinguished by the "aged persons" mentioned earlier (1 Tim. 5:1-2). There was a plurality of elders in each church (Titus 1:5). "Elder" therefore, is a general term for leaders in the church. And, although every minister is on "elder", not all elders were pastors or bishops or apostles (Acts 15:2, 4, 6, 22; etc.) Peter, on apostle, referred to himself as an "elder" (1 Peter 5:1).

How were Elders set in office!

It is a good feeling to have learned to set worthwhile goals and then be the master and manager of those goals, instead of becoming the slave to them.

God gives great joy as I am learning to balance the ongoing stretch to new horizons while also enjoying each precious day in ministry to its fullest. People who live in the Spirit of God are fun to be around. In Acts 14:23 Paul and Barnabas appointed elders for them in each church and, with prayer and fasting, committed them to the Lord, in whom they had put their trust. In Titus, Paul explained the purpose and function of Titus as Bishop in Crete. He wrote: "The reason I left you in Crete was that you might straighten out

---

5 ibid

what was left unfinished and appoint elders in every town, as I directed you" (Titus 1:5).

In the early Church, we find that Paul and Barnabas (apostles) ordained elders in every Church they established. Elders were never voted in office as most of our churches do today. Rather they were ordained by the apostles and their calling was confirmed by the congregation. Their work was to rule over the congregation and ensure its wellbeing. Elders worked in close relationship with the apostles and prophets who were the foundation layers.

Their ordination was for life, unless they were scripturally disqualified (See Acts 1:22, 10:42, 13:48, 16:4, 1Corn. 9:14, Heb.5:1, 8:3, Titus 1:5; James 5:14; etc.).

The Qualifications of an Elder

Before an elder could be chosen, he had to meet certain qualifications; for instance, he had to be a man of prayer (Acts 14:23). Prayer and fasting are two spiritual activities that are of paramount importance if any servant of the Lord is to be used by the Holy Spirit to the fullest capacity. In, addition, an elder had to be a man of the Word, one who studies and lives his life according to God's Word. (Num. 27:11-23, Deut. 1:16-18, 1 &2Tim)

He must be a person who can teach and minister the Word of God to his people. I have seen congregations over the years that are kept in spiritual poverty because their elders are poor teachers. If an elder cannot teach, he should get someone else to teach for him. It is a sin to keep God's sheep (people) starving. See Jer. 23:4; Eze.34:2; Mi. 3:11; Heb. 13:17.1Tim. 5:17: The elders who direct the affairs of the church well are worthy of double honor, especially those whose work is preaching and teaching" (1 Tim.5: 17).

1. An elder must have a genuine conversion experience, not just head knowledge of spiritual things. He must be one who walks in obedience to the Word of God (John 3:1-5). He also must be Spirit—filled (Acts 2:1-4). Elders who are not Spirit—filled constantly hinder God's move in their congregations. They are blind leaders (Eph.5:18, 1 Tim. 3:9, Titus 1:9).

2. An elder must be a person of integrity, of blameless and unquestionable character. An elder must be a good example to

others and free from scandals (2 Corn. 6:3, Gal. 2:11, Phil.2:15, 2 Peter 3:14).

Characteristics:

In 1 & 2 Timothy and Titus are Paul's last group of writings, called the "Pastoral Epistles" because they deal largely with:

1. Pastoral work of the Church
2. The duties of the Minister

They are written to give instructions to pastors in change of congregations. Their application is as good now as it was then. They are concerned with:

1. The Government of the Church
2. The appointment of its officers
3. The ordering of its worship
4. The Maintenance of its discipline
5. The safe-guarding of its doctrine
6. The care and wellbeing of its members

Although addressed to individuals (Timothy and Titus), they are concerned with public and not private affairs. The elders are in reality throughout, especially 2 Timothy, valedictory character.

Observations of Elder:

Based on literary grounds, the language of Pastorals (Elders) is non-Pauline they contain many words not found in his other writings and that the style is different. It must be remembered that Paul was a writer with a very wide vocabulary and master of many styles. He introduced many new words in all his epistles examples, (1 Corn. 12 & Chapter 14. Eph. 4 To 1 & 2Tim Titus, Phil 1).

The word 'Elder' as an adjectives meant 'an age man' or 'a person advanced in life'—he was set apart to administer justice, settle disputes, and guide the people of his charge. And therefore signifies that a person ordained to this office was elderly and therefore wise, mature and responsible enough to be entrusted with leadership roles. They would then and thus manifest certain capabilities and moral qualities and acquire weight, which would make them respected and valued. We find that throughout the New Testament

the word 'elder' is used interchangeably with the word 'bishop' which means an overseer in Greek. The growth and the well-being of a local Church is highly dependent on having the right and qualified people for this important office.

Contributor

In our Churches today, we have quite a significant number of people who have been placed into offices, without any prior training, or even more to the point, no training while in their positions. There has been too much of this in the past, and there is a great deal of it even in the present day. The result has been the lack of a sound understanding and a proper evaluation of the truth role. It is no wonder therefore, why people fail to live up to the roles that they have been called to fulfil.

It is often said that when you ask an Evangelist in the church "what is your role"? Very often the reply is that they do not know. There was no appreciation of the fact that the Holy Spirit guided the Church in the interpretation and development of the truth as it is revealed in the Word of God. The author of this book: "Practical Policy Making and Job Description in Christian Ministry and Mission", I have read some of his publications. I am delighted to write this contribution to a scholar who is willing to share his knowledge and develop younger ministers, pastors, teachers and even bishops and students also others working in the ministry alike.

Dr. A. P. Miller, a well-known Author, whose previous books includes "How to Manage Human Resources in Organizations", has once again, heeded the call of God to write to the Body of Christ to remind, to warn, and to exhort them of their responsibilities, and to be aware of not only their positions, or titles, but most important of all, their responsibility to God, to the people that they serve, and also to themselves.

In a time when church roles are the norm, church leaders, denominational staff, judicatory executives, and seminarians will want this book to help them "lead ministry and mission" in spiritual and healthy way. The Christian church should insist that those who are called to his or her varied ministries role be thoroughly educated or understand the relevant disciplines that an individual need to effectively carry out the work of ministry.

God bless you, and continue to write for God and His people.

P. Powell, BD. M. Min., D. Th.,

Head of Triumphant Bible College: Jamaica WI

Pastor of Triumphant Church of God, Jamaica WI

Chapter Thirteen

The Ministry of the Bishop

The word bishop is used a limited number of times in the New Testament, but it has significant implications for a proper understanding of leadership in the church. We have the noun EPISKOPOS which seem to appears about five times in the New Testament and means overseer, guardian and bishop. It is used in reference to Jesus Christ in {1 Peter 2:25} and in other places of individuals who have a function of leadership in the church {Acts 20:28; Phil.1:1; 1 Timothy 3:2; Titus 1:7}

For you were as sheep going astray but are now returned unto the Shepherd and Bishop of your souls {1 Peter 2:25AV}.

Take heed therefore unto yourselves, and to all the Flock over the which the Holy Spirit has made you overseers, to feed the Church of God which He has purchased with His Own Blood {Acts 20:28AV}. In this chapter from vv.27-30 bishop or overseer are told to shepherd the flock of God, by declaring the whole counsel of the Word of God {v.27}.

For I have not shunned to declare unto you all the Counsel of God {Acts 20:27AV}.

The reason is because there will arise false teachers who will seek to lead many astray {vv.29-30}

For I know this, that after my departing shall grievous wolves enter in among you, not sparing the flock. Also of your own selves shall men arise speaking perverse things, to draw away Disciples after them {Acts 20:29-30AV}.

The first responsibility God has given the bishop or overseer is to watch over the flock. The idea is one of spiritual alertness, being on watch, being ready.

Paul, a prisoner of Jesus Christ, and Timothy our brother, unto Philemon our dearly beloved, and fellow-labourer {Philemon 1:1AV}.

In writing to a local congregation or ministry, the church at Philippi, Paul addresses himself to the bishops or overseers {1:1}. It is inconceivable that Paul would have sent no greetings at all to the elders, who were in every church. This could be that the bishops, overseer and elders must be one and the same body of individuals.

This is a true saying, if a man desire the office of a bishop, he desires a good work. A Bishop then must be blameless the husband of one wife, vigilant, sober, of good behaviour, given to hospitality, apt to teach {1 Timothy 3:1-2 AV}.

Clearly, "bishop" {episkopos} refers to the function of the office, while "elder" {presbuteros} emphasizes the character of spiritually mature men of God. It was a term of respect and esteem the early church employed to describe its pastoral leaders, even though they were, on occasion, very young. And a character in all aspects of life, both personal and public.

This expresses also the idea that the bishop should demonstrate integrity in every area as Paul mentions. His life and reputation are of such a nature that he is not open to attack or censure. No fault can be found in him that would disqualify him from office or open him to discipline by the body {1 Timothy 5:19-20}.

Against an Elder receive not an accusation, but before two or three witnesses. Them who sin rebuke before all that others also may fear {1 Timothy 5:19-20AV}.

The bishop must be above reproach in his public life. He must be able to teach and hold firm to the message so that he can encourage others by sound doctrine and refute those who oppose it.

If any be blameless, the husband of one wife, having faithful children not accused of riot or unruly. For a Bishop must be blameless, as the steward of God not self-willed, not soon angry, not given to wine, no striker not given to filthy lucre; but a lover of hospitality, a lover of good men, sober, just, holy, temperate holding fast the faithful word as he has been taught that he may be able by sound doctrine both to exhort and to convince the gainsayers {Titus 1:6-9AV}.

We have also the verb episcope, which appears in {1 Timothy 3:1}; it means "bishoprick" {Acts 1:20}, "the office of a bishop" {1 Timothy 3:1} or "overseership". It refers to the position or office of bishop or overseer. It seems clear that a plurality of overseer as well as elders was the New Testament model, though flexibility apparently existed as to structure.

This is a true saying, if a man desire the office of a Bishop, he desires a good work {1 Timothy 3:1AV}. The same verb appears in {1 Peter 5:2}, which means to take care of, to oversee, or to care for.

Feed the flock of God which is among you, taking the oversight thereof, not by constraint, but willingly not for filthy lucre, but of a ready mind {1 Peter 5:2AV}.

A responsibility of the bishop is to shepherd the flock of God as instructed to you. To shepherd carries the idea of tending, caring for, feeding, protecting, and leading. All these tasks are involved in the bishop / overseer's service of ministry to the spiritual flock of God. Responsibility is not a compulsion but something that the bishop / overseer has entered into willingly.

The office of the bishop or overseer is both a great privilege and an awesome responsibility. The office of a bishop is a high ecclesiastical office which requires responsibility and authority. With responsibility comes accountability and the authority to function effectively. These two can be further summarized as follows:

1. Definite and clear-cut responsibilities should be assigned to each bishop. What causes a person who seems to have the ability to perform a given task to stop short of shouldering the responsibility for making that decisions?

2. Responsibility should always be coupled with corresponding authority. The point here is that the leader {bishop}, whether emerging from the local group, elected by the group, or appointed by a higher authority, must constantly take into account these variables, which to a great extent condition the results of church group activity.

The "office of a Bishop" is used in a variety of ways to define different functions, depending on the level of responsibility and scope of authority. Different churches, like the Anglicans, Catholics, and some Evangelical and Pentecostal churches use different designations for "the office of Bishop". The various functions may be defined and described as follows:

National Board of Bishops

This Apostolic Council, sometimes called Bishop Council, shall consist of all duly consecrated Bishops of the College who have not been appointed to the Executive Board of Bishops. Along with the Executive Board of Bishops, members of the Bishops Council make up the General Board of Bishops. The meetings of the General Board of Bishops shall be called "The Episcopal Session". More recently the church council of bishops has become more interested in group study and wants to train its leadership in the principles of group work. Since we claim to operate from a high motivation leading people to be more like Jesus Christ ought to appear at the top of most ministry priority lists.

In the church **bishop** is an ordained minister who holds the fullness of the teaching doctrine, governing churches in his areas, jurisdiction or diocese. In almost every definition the process of bishop in organization involves leaders, followers, members, subordinates, or constituents as they interact, create visions, become inspired, find meaning in their work and lives, and gain in trust and respect. In turn, the churches trace the origins of the office of bishop to the apostles, who it is believed, were endowed with a special charism by the Holy Spirit at Pentecost.

Each bishop behaves differently at different times because their perception of situations differs. Changed perceptions lead to changed behaviour. Some Bishops feel satisfied when they realize that their perception and consequent behaviour are considered correct in the eyes of the bishop group that name is given to. Because some Churches hold that the "College of Bishops" or "The Bishops Council" as a group is the successor of the "College of Apostles", the bishops of the Church in ecumenical council have the authority to govern the Church. However, the Church also holds that uniquely among the apostles Saint Peter was granted a role of leadership and authority, giving him the right to speak for the Church and making his leadership necessary for the completion of the College.

But we need to understand that not every bishop group operates in a vacuum. Its members bring to it certain attitudes and patterns of behaviour that they have cultivated as individuals and from their contact with other groups. Some may feel essentially involved in the success and future of the bishop group; others may be participating only because of compulsion. Some possess higher educational levels than others. Some may be wealthy, some almost poor.

The next generation of church leaders will need to lay more emphasis on more training or Christian education as a prerequisite for this office. This is necessary for the Bishop to be effective in ministering to the various people under his leadership. However, the office of Bishop is not conferred by College degree alone; one must be Spirit-filled and anointed for this office. It would seem however, that, in most churches, the success of the Bishop depends on the demography, the number of people in the area where he presides as bishop—not necessarily on being filled with or anointed by the Holy Spirit. We have observed, however, that the style, character, personality and experience of the bishop are also significant for success.

Because of their function as teachers of the faith, it is customary in some English-speaking countries, to add to the names of bishops the post nominal title of "D.D."(Doctor of Divinity) and to refer to them with the title "Doctor". In some churches—especially in the Roman Catholic Church—only a bishop or any other church dignitary of high rank may grant imprimaturs for theological books, certifying that they are free from doctrinal or moral error; this is an expression of the teaching authority, and education responsibility of the bishop.

We need bishops who have more than doctoral degrees, we need bishops who are filled with the Holy Spirit, with personal integrity and exemplary character. A bishop must be blames, according to Apostle Paul {1 Tim.3:1-2}. He must demonstrate by the consistency of his lifestyle and unquestionable dedication to service that Christ lives in him.

PRELATE BISHOP—A Bishop heading a small diocese called Prelature. In this context, the word "communication", describes how this bishop members relate to one another—how they transmit their ideas, values, feelings, and attitudes toward matters which the bishop group decides. Of course, some communication patterns in a bishop group will be nonverbal.

Primate in some Churches: A primate is usually the bishop of the oldest diocese of a nation; the title is one of honour. While others use it as the highest office within their church fellowship. Of course some of the standards are not always written, and they may not always show high quality; but all prelate groups embrace some mutually accepted determination of conduct. Formal prelate groups may use formal procedures, and informal prelate groups, informal procedures; but all prelate bishops operate with some pattern of function. The effectiveness of the prelate is linked to its goal achievement. In turn, goal achievement is affected by goal clarification.

The concept of "calling" and "gifting" remind us that every Christian is a candidate and a potential church leader. It is the Lord who calls and equips His people for ministry—at all levels; and those who are called are expected to meet the essential prerequisite for the office of a bishop {See: 1 tim.3:1-7; Tit.1:6-9}. Moreover, a bishop must consistently walk with the Lord, through a regular prayer life and God-centered living.

PATRIARCH BISHOP-Bishop heading an Ancient Church called Patriachy whose roots reach to the time of the Apostles and their immediate successors. The evaluation of the patriarch bishop should not only look at the past but plan the future on the basis of the past. Some call the Prelate and Patriarch Bishop the Chief Executive officer of the church, while others call it the President of the fellowship. This patriarch bishop can express his opinions honestly, expecting that other colleagues {or fellow bishops} will receive and consider them fairly.

Because of the emphasis that has been placed on patriarch bishop in various realms of study, such as religion, sociology, psychology, and education, in the past two decades, some people tend to think of this group work as a panacea for all of the problems church faces. Of course we can't do this until we first discover or identify the suitable spiritual climate in which to grow and mature both bishop and members. The Bishops need to constantly "study to shew" themselves "approved unto God" {2 Tim.2:15}, and strive to develop their spiritual gifting, leadership skills, natural talents and abilities. This will greatly enhance their effectiveness in leadership and also help them to maintain a closer walk with God.

Diocesan or Jurisdictional or Provincial bishops: These bishops exhibit a conscious altruism and receptive teamwork which are actually contagious to new ministers. Making the traditional role of a bishop is to act as head of a diocese or eparchy. Dioceses vary considerably in geographical size and population. A wide variety of dioceses world around the which received the Christian faith early are rather compact in size, while those in areas more recently evangelized, tend to be much larger and more populous. Some bishops surrender selfishness to the achievement of organization goals, but they do not sacrifice individuality on the altar of collectiveness. Sometimes self-inspection on the part of the church organization and evaluation of its motives and objectives are valid procedures, for they have the oversight of an Apostolic Areas.

These bishops are known to have consecrating and dedicating served faithfully, willingly, and sometimes sacrificially. They are entrusted with the care of a local church diocese. The bishop is responsible for teaching, governing, and the faithful, of his diocese, sharing these duties with the priests or pastors and deacons who serve under him. The values of the presentation of joint thinking on a controversial issue has more authority and can evoke more respect than the attitude of one person, regardless of that person's role or title. Perhaps it is necessary at this point to say the bishop serves as the "chief shepherd" (spiritual leader) of the diocese and has responsibility for the pastoral care of all members living within his ecclesiastical and ritual jurisdiction. A bishop is to have a special concern for pastors or priests, listening to them, using them as counsellors, ensuring that they are adequately provided for in every way, and defending their rights set forth in the Code of Canon Law. Though various structures appear in different types of Christian organizations, the actual function of bishop boards and committees takes on a striking similarity.

TITULARY BISHOP—He maintains the ceremonial title of an extinct (Diocesan Bishop) Diocese. The word "titular is used of a title "in name only". It is used in the Roman Catholic Church to designate "any of certain churches in Rome to whom cardinals or bishops are attached as their nominal incumbents". It is in essence, the bearer of a nominal {not in reality} office {from Latin "titulus"—title}. No doubt the various functions of titular bishop could be categorized in any number of ways, but one of the clearest would be to specify the bishop's relationship to the policies of the church. Since a typical Diocese only has one Bishop, the title of the Diocese belongs to the head-bishop alone. You can see immediately the balance of power and catapults one person into a frightening position. In some churches, different guidelines are given for different levels of bishops.

In my opinion, the same guidelines should prevail also in board of bishops at all levels. Unless we understand what we're trying to do, we'll end up with frustrated clergy men and frustrated lay members. Here we have a two-sided coin. Obviously we want quality personnel to head the church diocese as bishop. That does not necessarily mean this people are more spiritual than the local pastors. But what is needed is someone who understands team leadership development even if he or she is not the highest educated in the organization. There must be a balance in the recruiting and retaining of leaders. Having thought through this a great deal as a pastor of a local church ministry, I have concluded I am looking for at least four basic qualities in my leadership team and also my leadership covering.

1. Spiritual Maturity. Since we are on a journey which leads to the ultimate goal of perfection in heaven, not on earth.

2. Leadership Skills. Leadership is learned behaviour, but I'd like to at least start with some behavioural level or skill—some basic skills for leadership which also affect behaviour.

3. Learning Potential. Here we must consider intelligence, willingness, and, if possible, even eagerness to learn and move forward in the challenges of Christian ministry.

4. Cooperative Attitude. People who cannot get along with each other in ministry have little chance of getting along with a different set of people.

AUXILIARY BISHOP—If one diocese increases its membership, activities and number of Pastors and resources, the services of one bishop becomes insufficient. And now the appointment of Auxiliary Bishop is valid. Auxiliary comes from the Latin word "Auxilium" which means "help". An Auxiliary Bishop means "Helper Bishop". In some Pentecostal churches and ministries, the word "Overseer" or "Superintendent" is used for this office—though both words come from the same Greek word for "bishop". **Auxiliary bishop** is a full-time assistant to a diocesan bishop. Auxiliaries are titular bishops without the right of succession, who assist the diocesan bishop in a variety of ways and are usually appointed as vicars general or Episcopal vicars of the diocese in which they serve. The bishop can be Administrative Officer of the church to a specific department or auxiliary.

These auxiliary bishops need to clearly understand their specific roles and tailor their programmes to their rate of growth. And as they grow, they can be elevated as full-fledged bishops. The recognition and elevation of a deserving auxiliary bishop does not only motivate him it does create a healthy environment for team ministry to flourish. The church organization that is able to employ a full time bishop certainly benefits from his leadership in this area.

Such bishops can be recommended for fulltime ministry, depending on the numerical strength and financial resources of the church. Any church that is capable of employing such bishops on fulltime will certainly benefit immensely from their experiences, wisdom, maturity, faithfulness and leadership expertise. They will be better in many respects for the church than those going the church from outside. Moreover, they will be of great assets to the church in several ways; they will be useful in training and mentoring pastors and other potential auxiliary bishops. Thus the church can grow spiritually and numerically, as more leaders are trained and more churches planted.

SUFFRAGAN BISHOP—is a bishop subordinate to a metropolitan bishop, diocesan bishop or an archbishop. The word is from the Latin word "Suffragium", which means "assistance". It is used of any bishop of a diocese "subordinate to and assisting his superior archbishop or metropolitan".[6] **Suffragan bishop** leads a diocese within an ecclesiastical province other than the principal diocese, the metropolitan archdiocese. The Suffragan Bishop, like other bishops, must be highly qualified and highly responsible to serve the church in this capacity. Apart from genuinely being called and spiritually equipped for leadership, he must understand the difference between "work" and "office" and strive to maintain a healthy balance. His role is essentially "supportive" in relation to other ministers. A faithful suffragan bishop who has consistently serval the church can become a cathedral bishop, if such opportunity arises.

Perhaps one of the key challenges of a bishop is the proper understanding and effective management of conflict within the church organization. Apart from being called and spiritually equipped, the church leader should be trained in counselling, and should properly understand human nature and interrelationships between the people and the church.

---

6 The Collins Dictionary of the English Language, Glasgow: William Collins Sons & Co. Ltd., 1989, p.1523

1.The Collins Dictionary of the English Language, Glasgow: William Collins Sons & Co. Ltd., 1989, p.1523

ARCHDIOCESAN BISHOP—He is the bishop who is to head of an **ARCHDIOCESE {the diocese of an archbishop}** **ARCHDIOCESE** is bigger than a Diocese. It is called "Mother Diocese" because sometimes a new Diocese comes from the Archdiocese. In the Anglican Church, "Archbishop" is the bishop with the highest rank. The Archbishop of Canterbury is the most senior clergy of the church. In the Roman Catholic Church, however, "Archbishop" is lower in rank than the "Cardinal" next to the pope. In some Pentecostal churches and ministries, the title "Archbishop" is used for the most senior clergy. This is the "bishop" among bishops. Others prefer "Presiding Bishop" or "Chief Bishop" or "General Overseer" etc. The function of an Archbishop carries enormous responsibilities. And, as the Bible says, "To whom much is given, much is required" {Luke 12:48}. To function effectively, therefore, the leader in this category needs to delegate responsibilities to his subordinate bishops.

In many Christian organizations the delegation process seems complicated by some leader's constant dealing with other bishops in the same group to take a task and carry it out even though such authority may be consistent. But difficult though it may be, delegation stands central to leadership roles carried out by bishop, pastors, associate staff, and other team leaders. In another sense, however, the leader can never delegate accountability.

Metropolitan archbishop is an archbishop with minor jurisdiction over an ecclesiastical province; in practice this amounts to presiding at meetings and overseeing a diocese which has no bishop. In Eastern Catholicism a metropolitan may also be the head of an autocephalous, or autonomous church when the number of adherents of that tradition is small. In the Latin Church, metropolitans are always archbishops; in many Eastern churches, the title is "metropolitan," with some of these churches using "archbishop" as a separate office. Amazing as it seems, one can be placed into this office only to deal theoretically with issues and therefore pays little more than lip service to the actual functions that make good and godly leadership possible.

Coadjutor bishop is a bishop who is given almost equal authority to that of the diocesan bishop; he has special faculties and the right to succeed the incumbent diocesan bishop. The appointment of coadjutors is seen as a means of providing for continuity of church leadership.

Dynamic forces operate within human personality that produce profound effects upon our interactions with other people on the team. Until recent times, there was the possibility of a coadjutor bishop not having the right of succession. This clearly implies that succession is not automatic, but based primarily on qualifications. In some cases, the judgment or decision of the Body of Bishops plays a crucial role. However, under normal conditions, a faithful Coadjutor bishop succeeds the diocesan bishop.

Retired bishops. When a diocesan bishop or auxiliary bishop retires, he is given the honorary title of "Emeritus" of his last see, that is, archbishop emeritus, bishop emeritus, or auxiliary bishop emeritus of the see. For the (arch)bishop of a diocese, "emeritus" is inserted into the title for the last diocese that the (arch)bishop occupied. An example in usage would be: "Most Reverend John Jones, Bishop Emeritus of the Diocese of Allan-town." For a cardinal, who does not cease to be a cardinal and a bishop, though no longer bishop of a see, it would be: "Cardinal James Smith, Archbishop Emeritus of the Archdiocese of Allan-City".

The word "emeritus" comes from the Latin word "merere", which denotes to derive, to merit. It is usually a title for retired people or those who are honourably discharged from fulltime service; they retain this title on an honourably basis. Presiding Bishop that has stepped down because of illness or other holy reasons is called Emeritus. Though retired, these Senior Clergy can still be useful to the church. They can serve as mentors to younger ministers.

Cardinal Bishop is a member of the clergy appointed by the Pope to serve in the College of Cardinals. Under canon law, a man appointed a cardinal must normally be a bishop, or accept ordination as a bishop, but may seek papal permission to decline such ordination. Most cardinals are already bishops when appointed, the majority being archbishops of important archdioceses or patriarchates, others already serving as titular bishops in the Roman Curia. Recent popes have appointed a few priests most of them renowned theologians, to the College of Cardinals, and these have been permitted to decline Episcopal ordination.

Contributor

The author of this book: "Practical Policy Making and Job Description in Christian Ministry and Mission", we met face to face almost four years, and prior to our meeting I had read some of his publications. I am delighted to write this contribution to a scholar who is willing to share his knowledge and develop younger ministers, pastors, teachers and even bishops and students also others working in the ministry alike.

In his book he highlights the job description of each department and this is very vital in churches of all sizes and locations. His ideas are very dynamic because any organization that is resistant to change will not develop and eventually die. Christ wants His Church to grow and be fruitful.

The book reveals most of the practicalities of ministry and is very helpful because of the detailed accounts provided for each department of the church. Dr. Allan Miller, throughout this book, has been consistently practical in every title featured and makes difficult issues clear, therefore enabling the reader to understand without any complexity.

I have also observed that Dr. Miller, in all his years of lecturing has demonstrated clarity in his writing, headings and sub headings, which allows the readers to understand his points of view. While there are many things a minister learns along the road in caring for the flock of the Lord, this book helps to facilitate this learning process. Rev Dr. Allan Miller is presently lecturing at our Bible College in East London, and he is well respected by both students and fellow lecturers.

From all what I have highlighted and more, I am convinced that readers will discover for themselves that this publication will be enormously useful in assisting in understanding each individual role in the Body of Christ. I am pleased to recommend this book to all theological students, all in leadership in Christian churches, ministerial training centers, or colleges and universities alike to the glory of the Lord.

Isaac Ojutalayo, BA. M. Th., D. D., D. Min.,

Head of All Nation Bible College and Theological Studies: London

Bishop of Cherubim & Seraphim Church, London: England.

Conclusion

The twenty-first-century Church must respond to its challenges, just like business must respond to its competitive world. Revolutionary changes are occurring in the world today that will forever alter the way Churches meet the needs of a lost world. In government, new ideas are replacing long time traditional approaches to problem-solving. Schools, Churches and Families are struggling with similar fundamental changes. These changes are so profound they sometimes seem over-whelming. Christian leaders who are out of touch with these changes will fast become obsolete.

Today's organizations are reeling from the human impacts of the changes that have been forced on them by technology, international competition, and demographics. Each of these changes will force people to let go of their old worlds, leave them in the neutral zone for an extended period, and then call on them to learn new behaviours and develop new attitudes. Once again, key figures in this vision-implanting process are those in Church leadership. With this attitude deeply instilled in the heart of every Christian Minister, a wonderful thing happens in the life of the Church.

This studies offers all levels of ministers and Church leaders both inspirational and instructive insights into those key foundational subject areas necessary for establishing a local Church with an effective world vision and outreach. It consists of a progressive series of teaching which provide a concise yet comprehensive apostolic foundation for Church leadership desiring both local growth and extra local Church expansion. The principles contained within this book have been proven successful in the life and ministry of the author. This study is written to present some of the essential foundation stones and building material necessary for the New Testament Church to fulfil its mission.

Church leaders and members alike are showing a growing sensitivity to the need for the work of the Church to "be done decently and in order" in accordance with Pauline theology (1 Corinthians 14:40). The awareness of Church leaders of the importance of the administrative function and the growth of this strategic field of Church leadership has highlighted the need for a comprehensive, conceptual framework.

This research challenges the status quo (i.e., doing things the same old way) and proposes a paradigmatic shift in thinking about ecclesiastical leadership. It calls leaders to become transformational leaders, answering this challenge is necessary to avoid catastrophic, misguided, ill-informed, or incapable leadership of the twenty-first-century Church.

This study has attempted to provide readers with a pragmatic and comprehensive approach to addressing the human aspects of change. Why should our organization change at all? Change is resulting in dramatic improvements in service, huge reductions in operating expenses, and enormous leaps in revenue and profits. Even the most carefully planned organizational changes can fail if individuals are not taken into consideration. There is nothing more fundamental or necessary in today's world than change.

The important thing is not methodology, but getting hold of God's vision, getting hold of the life behind the Church's Ministry and Mission. The nature of leadership is missional, not institutional. The task is not to focus on revising old structures, having more effective meetings, developing better goals, and involving more people in more committees.

It's a valuable system for passing down specialized skills, nuances, and traditions that almost anyone can benefit from. Church Leaders need an administrative style of leadership. The equipping, enabling approach becomes his or her style of leadership. It is a management style. This concept reflects the foundational philosophy of this research. Leadership Implementing Positive Change in Church: it is assumed that there is a universality of principles between fields of implementing changes in various sectors of society.

Congregational change does not happen by gathering the larger circles of active, inactive, or community members and offering education or training about the needed change. It begins at the heart of the congregation, within the leadership circle. Leaders need to do the hard and necessary up—front work to understand and develop their own spirits, thoughts, and behaviours, which provide the health and the strength that will enable the congregation to live well and aspire to a greater and deeper relationship with Christ. But beyond providing education and training, leaders will also need to model the change. They will need to be seen participating in and practicing the new behaviours that are required. Taking a new position, offering a different opinion, experimenting with a new programme idea, or behaviour does not need to be seen as an offence. Leading a congregation in change will inevitably take us into an encounter with differences and conflicts.

To the contrary, there is the clear implication that these things should be happening simultaneously and are of equal importance. Most churches have fashioned themselves after business organizations—leaders at the top, members at the bottom. Churches should abolish this hierarchy by using teams, task forces, liaison roles, and by integrating roles. A congregation may need to make both formal and informal adjustments to encourage pastor participation. In fact, leaders and pastors may need to work very hard at system changes that nurture interaction between members and leaders.

I am fully aware that, in every profession or field of endeavour, whether secular or religious, changes are difficult to implement, especially when a thing has been done in certain ways for a very long time. Naturally, human beings, by their nature, do not adopt easily to changes in methodology. But the results of positive changes, especially in Church leadership, are very beneficial, though painful initially.

Many Christians are afraid to apply business principles to the Church. They are more comfortable about applying Christian principles to business. To such, I would admonish to prayerfully reconsider their methodology, in the light of modern standards. They should allow their mind to be flexible, rather than being fixed and settled in their ways.

Upon completion of a thorough study of this book, students of different fields should be able to perform satisfactorily certain types of behaviour. None of us are fully equipped to excel in life. Our weaknesses, blind spots, limited capabilities, and lack of experience all point to one thing—interdependence.

Which is why connecting with others plays such an indispensable role in healthy development. And, in addition to enhancing the leader's own potential in all of life's growth areas (spiritual, emotional, professional, relational, etc.), the things he will discover will equip him to help others as well.

It is my hope that, through this book, the reader will appreciate some of the dynamic possibilities for human achievement, under God, which might be wrought by persons working together decently and in order, in accordance with tested and proven principles. This study is an attempt to present major elements of such a theoretical framework.

It is essential that treasurers need special gifts and skills. They also need moral and spiritual qualities. They need to be of good reputation honest and dependable, with spiritual maturity, dedication to Christ, have a good love for their fellows and a genuine desire to serve both.

But to find the perfect treasurer is not feasibly, this has not yet been discovered—any more than has the same perfect minister! Some are in fact, far from ideal and often they would be the first to admit it and that goes for all the ministers too.

Therefore, the church should accept their Treasurers, encourage, support and equip them, and believe that God can and will use them. This is only when God comes into the equation and makes the result very much different from what otherwise would be the case.

Allan P. Miller, D. Min. Th., D. R. Ed., Ph.D. (Hon. D. C. C)

Other books of the Author

- How to manage Human Resource in Organizations
- Pastoral Care and Counselling
- Dealing with the Sheep, Goats, Wolves and Watchdog in Ministry
- Four Basic Steps for an Effective Ministry
- Where is God?
- The Philosophical and Theological Nature of the Church's Ministry and Mission
- The Philosophy of Christian Education in the Pentecostal Community
- Practical Wisdom for Excellence in Ministry & Mission